This ADHD Symptom Tracker

Belongs to:

_____

_____

ADHD Medication and
BEHAVIOR Tracker

Week of: ___/___/___

	M	T	W	T	F	S	S
Initiate Social Contact							
Social Contact Results							
Medication Time & Dose							
Maintained Daily Routine							
Sleep and Rest hours							
Healthy Diet							
Exercise / Activity							
BEHAVIOR TRACKER							
Became Irritable	1 — 10	1 — 10	1 — 10	1 — 10	1 — 10	1 — 10	1 — 10
Felt Agitated	1 — 10	1 — 10	1 — 10	1 — 10	1 — 10	1 — 10	1 — 10
Unable to concentrate	1 — 10	1 — 10	1 — 10	1 — 10	1 — 10	1 — 10	1 — 10
Memory Loss	1 — 10	1 — 10	1 — 10	1 — 10	1 — 10	1 — 10	1 — 10
Energy Level	1 — 10	1 — 10	1 — 10	1 — 10	1 — 10	1 — 10	1 — 10
Kept Focus	1 — 10	1 — 10	1 — 10	1 — 10	1 — 10	1 — 10	1 — 10
Able to complete tasks	1 — 10	1 — 10	1 — 10	1 — 10	1 — 10	1 — 10	1 — 10
Motivation level	1 — 10	1 — 10	1 — 10	1 — 10	1 — 10	1 — 10	1 — 10
Healthy appetite	1 — 10	1 — 10	1 — 10	1 — 10	1 — 10	1 — 10	1 — 10
Physical symptoms:							
• Headache	1 — 10	1 — 10	1 — 10	1 — 10	1 — 10	1 — 10	1 — 10
• Lethargy	1 — 10	1 — 10	1 — 10	1 — 10	1 — 10	1 — 10	1 — 10
• Nausea	1 — 10	1 — 10	1 — 10	1 — 10	1 — 10	1 — 10	1 — 10
• Other							
Notes							

REJECTION DYSPHORIA WORKSHEET

Date: _____

Time: _____

Where did the social interaction take place?
What exact words were said and by whom?
Then what exactly happened?

What did I think and how did I feel before I reacted to that?

What words did I use to respond? What was the effect of those words on the other person involved?

What was the outcome of this encounter?

If I felt rejected, how could I have reframed my thoughts to ward off that feeling?

Did I learn anything specific about myself or the other person? Any ideas how to better approach my next social interaction?

ADHD Medication and
BEHAVIOR Tracker

Week of:

____/____/____

	M	T	W	T	F	S	S
Initiate Social Contact							
Social Contact Results							
Medication Time & Dose							
Maintained Daily Routine							
Sleep and Rest hours							
Healthy Diet							
Exercise / Activity							

BEHAVIOR TRACKER

	M	T	W	T	F	S	S
Became Irritable	1 – 10	1 – 10	1 – 10	1 – 10	1 – 10	1 – 10	1 – 10
Felt Agitated	1 – 10	1 – 10	1 – 10	1 – 10	1 – 10	1 – 10	1 – 10
Unable to concentrate	1 – 10	1 – 10	1 – 10	1 – 10	1 – 10	1 – 10	1 – 10
Memory Loss	1 – 10	1 – 10	1 – 10	1 – 10	1 – 10	1 – 10	1 – 10
Energy Level	1 – 10	1 – 10	1 – 10	1 – 10	1 – 10	1 – 10	1 – 10
Kept Focus	1 – 10	1 – 10	1 – 10	1 – 10	1 – 10	1 – 10	1 – 10
Able to complete tasks	1 – 10	1 – 10	1 – 10	1 – 10	1 – 10	1 – 10	1 – 10
Motivation level	1 – 10	1 – 10	1 – 10	1 – 10	1 – 10	1 – 10	1 – 10
Healthy appetite	1 – 10	1 – 10	1 – 10	1 – 10	1 – 10	1 – 10	1 – 10
Physical symptoms:							
• Headache	1 – 10	1 – 10	1 – 10	1 – 10	1 – 10	1 – 10	1 – 10
• Lethargy	1 – 10	1 – 10	1 – 10	1 – 10	1 – 10	1 – 10	1 – 10
• Nausea	1 – 10	1 – 10	1 – 10	1 – 10	1 – 10	1 – 10	1 – 10
• Other							
Notes							

REJECTION DYSPHORIA WORKSHEET

Date:
_____

Time:
_____

Where did the social interaction take place?
What exact words were said and by whom?
Then what exactly happened?

What did I think and how did I feel before I reacted to that?

What words did I use to respond? What was the effect of those words on the other person involved?

What was the outcome of this encounter?

If I felt rejected, how could I have reframed my thoughts to ward off that feeling?

Did I learn anything specific about myself or the other person? Any ideas how to better approach my next social interaction?

ADHD Medication and
BEHAVIOR Tracker

Week of: ___ / ___ / ___

	M	T	W	T	F	S	S
Initiate Social Contact							
Social Contact Results							
Medication Time & Dose							
Maintained Daily Routine							
Sleep and Rest hours							
Healthy Diet							
Exercise / Activity							

BEHAVIOR TRACKER

	M	T	W	T	F	S	S
Became Irritable	1 — 10	1 — 10	1 — 10	1 — 10	1 — 10	1 — 10	1 — 10
Felt Agitated	1 — 10	1 — 10	1 — 10	1 — 10	1 — 10	1 — 10	1 — 10
Unable to concentrate	1 — 10	1 — 10	1 — 10	1 — 10	1 — 10	1 — 10	1 — 10
Memory Loss	1 — 10	1 — 10	1 — 10	1 — 10	1 — 10	1 — 10	1 — 10
Energy Level	1 — 10	1 — 10	1 — 10	1 — 10	1 — 10	1 — 10	1 — 10
Kept Focus	1 — 10	1 — 10	1 — 10	1 — 10	1 — 10	1 — 10	1 — 10
Able to complete tasks	1 — 10	1 — 10	1 — 10	1 — 10	1 — 10	1 — 10	1 — 10
Motivation level	1 — 10	1 — 10	1 — 10	1 — 10	1 — 10	1 — 10	1 — 10
Healthy appetite	1 — 10	1 — 10	1 — 10	1 — 10	1 — 10	1 — 10	1 — 10
Physical symptoms:							
• Headache	1 — 10	1 — 10	1 — 10	1 — 10	1 — 10	1 — 10	1 — 10
• Lethargy	1 — 10	1 — 10	1 — 10	1 — 10	1 — 10	1 — 10	1 — 10
• Nausea	1 — 10	1 — 10	1 — 10	1 — 10	1 — 10	1 — 10	1 — 10
• Other							
Notes							

REJECTION DYSPHORIA WORKSHEET

Date: _____

Time: _____

Where did the social interaction take place?
What exact words were said and by whom?
Then what exactly happened?

What did I think and how did I feel before I reacted to that?

What words did I use to respond? What was the effect of those words on the other person involved?

What was the outcome of this encounter?

If I felt rejected, how could I have reframed my thoughts to ward off that feeling?

Did I learn anything specific about myself or the other person? Any ideas how to better approach my next social interaction?

ADHD Medication and
BEHAVIOR Tracker

Week of:

___/___/___

	M	T	W	T	F	S	S
Initiate Social Contact							
Social Contact Results							
Medication Time & Dose							
Maintained Daily Routine							
Sleep and Rest hours							
Healthy Diet							
Exercise / Activity							

BEHAVIOR TRACKER

	M	T	W	T	F	S	S
Became Irritable	1 — 10	1 — 10	1 — 10	1 — 10	1 — 10	1 — 10	1 — 10
Felt Agitated	1 — 10	1 — 10	1 — 10	1 — 10	1 — 10	1 — 10	1 — 10
Unable to concentrate	1 — 10	1 — 10	1 — 10	1 — 10	1 — 10	1 — 10	1 — 10
Memory Loss	1 — 10	1 — 10	1 — 10	1 — 10	1 — 10	1 — 10	1 — 10
Energy Level	1 — 10	1 — 10	1 — 10	1 — 10	1 — 10	1 — 10	1 — 10
Kept Focus	1 — 10	1 — 10	1 — 10	1 — 10	1 — 10	1 — 10	1 — 10
Able to complete tasks	1 — 10	1 — 10	1 — 10	1 — 10	1 — 10	1 — 10	1 — 10
Motivation level	1 — 10	1 — 10	1 — 10	1 — 10	1 — 10	1 — 10	1 — 10
Healthy appetite	1 — 10	1 — 10	1 — 10	1 — 10	1 — 10	1 — 10	1 — 10
Physical symptoms:							
• Headache	1 — 10	1 — 10	1 — 10	1 — 10	1 — 10	1 — 10	1 — 10
• Lethargy	1 — 10	1 — 10	1 — 10	1 — 10	1 — 10	1 — 10	1 — 10
• Nausea	1 — 10	1 — 10	1 — 10	1 — 10	1 — 10	1 — 10	1 — 10
• Other							
Notes							

REJECTION DYSPHORIA WORKSHEET

Date:
_____

Time:
_____

Where did the social interaction take place?
What exact words were said and by whom?
Then what exactly happened?

What did I think and how did I feel before I reacted to that?

What words did I use to respond? What was the effect of those words on the other person involved?

What was the outcome of this encounter?

If I felt rejected, how could I have reframed my thoughts to ward off that feeling?

Did I learn anything specific about myself or the other person?
Any ideas how to better approach my next social interaction?

ADHD Medication and
BEHAVIOR Tracker

Week of: ____/____/____

	M	T	W	T	F	S	S
Initiate Social Contact							
Social Contact Results							
Medication Time & Dose							
Maintained Daily Routine							
Sleep and Rest hours							
Healthy Diet							
Exercise / Activity							

BEHAVIOR TRACKER

	M	T	W	T	F	S	S
Became Irritable	1 — 10	1 — 10	1 — 10	1 — 10	1 — 10	1 — 10	1 — 10
Felt Agitated	1 — 10	1 — 10	1 — 10	1 — 10	1 — 10	1 — 10	1 — 10
Unable to concentrate	1 — 10	1 — 10	1 — 10	1 — 10	1 — 10	1 — 10	1 — 10
Memory Loss	1 — 10	1 — 10	1 — 10	1 — 10	1 — 10	1 — 10	1 — 10
Energy Level	1 — 10	1 — 10	1 — 10	1 — 10	1 — 10	1 — 10	1 — 10
Kept Focus	1 — 10	1 — 10	1 — 10	1 — 10	1 — 10	1 — 10	1 — 10
Able to complete tasks	1 — 10	1 — 10	1 — 10	1 — 10	1 — 10	1 — 10	1 — 10
Motivation level	1 — 10	1 — 10	1 — 10	1 — 10	1 — 10	1 — 10	1 — 10
Healthy appetite	1 — 10	1 — 10	1 — 10	1 — 10	1 — 10	1 — 10	1 — 10
Physical symptoms:							
• Headache	1 — 10	1 — 10	1 — 10	1 — 10	1 — 10	1 — 10	1 — 10
• Lethargy	1 — 10	1 — 10	1 — 10	1 — 10	1 — 10	1 — 10	1 — 10
• Nausea	1 — 10	1 — 10	1 — 10	1 — 10	1 — 10	1 — 10	1 — 10
• Other							

Notes

REJECTION DYSPHORIA WORKSHEET

Date: _____

Time: _____

Where did the social interaction take place?
What exact words were said and by whom?
Then what exactly happened?

What did I think and how did I feel before I reacted to that?

What words did I use to respond? What was the effect of those words on the other person involved?

What was the outcome of this encounter?

If I felt rejected, how could I have reframed my thoughts to ward off that feeling?

Did I learn anything specific about myself or the other person? Any ideas how to better approach my next social interaction?

ADHD Medication and
BEHAVIOR Tracker

Week of:

___ / ___ / ___

	M	T	W	T	F	S	S
Initiate Social Contact							
Social Contact Results							
Medication Time & Dose							
Maintained Daily Routine							
Sleep and Rest hours							
Healthy Diet							
Exercise / Activity							

BEHAVIOR TRACKER

	M	T	W	T	F	S	S
Became Irritable	1 — 10	1 — 10	1 — 10	1 — 10	1 — 10	1 — 10	1 — 10
Felt Agitated	1 — 10	1 — 10	1 — 10	1 — 10	1 — 10	1 — 10	1 — 10
Unable to concentrate	1 — 10	1 — 10	1 — 10	1 — 10	1 — 10	1 — 10	1 — 10
Memory Loss	1 — 10	1 — 10	1 — 10	1 — 10	1 — 10	1 — 10	1 — 10
Energy Level	1 — 10	1 — 10	1 — 10	1 — 10	1 — 10	1 — 10	1 — 10
Kept Focus	1 — 10	1 — 10	1 — 10	1 — 10	1 — 10	1 — 10	1 — 10
Able to complete tasks	1 — 10	1 — 10	1 — 10	1 — 10	1 — 10	1 — 10	1 — 10
Motivation level	1 — 10	1 — 10	1 — 10	1 — 10	1 — 10	1 — 10	1 — 10
Healthy appetite	1 — 10	1 — 10	1 — 10	1 — 10	1 — 10	1 — 10	1 — 10
Physical symptoms:							
• Headache	1 — 10	1 — 10	1 — 10	1 — 10	1 — 10	1 — 10	1 — 10
• Lethargy	1 — 10	1 — 10	1 — 10	1 — 10	1 — 10	1 — 10	1 — 10
• Nausea	1 — 10	1 — 10	1 — 10	1 — 10	1 — 10	1 — 10	1 — 10
• Other							
Notes							

REJECTION DYSPHORIA WORKSHEET

Date: _____

Time: _____

Where did the social interaction take place?
What exact words were said and by whom?
Then what exactly happened?

What did I think and how did I feel before I reacted to that?

What words did I use to respond? What was the effect of those words on the other person involved?

What was the outcome of this encounter?

If I felt rejected, how could I have reframed my thoughts to ward off that feeling?

Did I learn anything specific about myself or the other person? Any ideas how to better approach my next social interaction?

ADHD Medication and
BEHAVIOR Tracker

Week of: ____/____/____

	M	T	W	T	F	S	S
Initiate Social Contact							
Social Contact Results							
Medication Time & Dose							
Maintained Daily Routine							
Sleep and Rest hours							
Healthy Diet							
Exercise / Activity							

BEHAVIOR TRACKER

	M	T	W	T	F	S	S
Became Irritable	1 — 10	1 — 10	1 — 10	1 — 10	1 — 10	1 — 10	1 — 10
Felt Agitated	1 — 10	1 — 10	1 — 10	1 — 10	1 — 10	1 — 10	1 — 10
Unable to concentrate	1 — 10	1 — 10	1 — 10	1 — 10	1 — 10	1 — 10	1 — 10
Memory Loss	1 — 10	1 — 10	1 — 10	1 — 10	1 — 10	1 — 10	1 — 10
Energy Level	1 — 10	1 — 10	1 — 10	1 — 10	1 — 10	1 — 10	1 — 10
Kept Focus	1 — 10	1 — 10	1 — 10	1 — 10	1 — 10	1 — 10	1 — 10
Able to complete tasks	1 — 10	1 — 10	1 — 10	1 — 10	1 — 10	1 — 10	1 — 10
Motivation level	1 — 10	1 — 10	1 — 10	1 — 10	1 — 10	1 — 10	1 — 10
Healthy appetite	1 — 10	1 — 10	1 — 10	1 — 10	1 — 10	1 — 10	1 — 10
Physical symptoms:							
• Headache	1 — 10	1 — 10	1 — 10	1 — 10	1 — 10	1 — 10	1 — 10
• Lethargy	1 — 10	1 — 10	1 — 10	1 — 10	1 — 10	1 — 10	1 — 10
• Nausea	1 — 10	1 — 10	1 — 10	1 — 10	1 — 10	1 — 10	1 — 10
• Other							
Notes							

REJECTION DYSPHORIA WORKSHEET

Date:
_____

Time:
_____

Where did the social interaction take place?
What exact words were said and by whom?
Then what exactly happened?

What did I think and how did I feel before I reacted to that?

What words did I use to respond?
What was the effect of those words on the other person involved?

What was the outcome of this encounter?

If I felt rejected, how could I have reframed my thoughts to ward off that feeling?

Did I learn anything specific about myself or the other person?
Any ideas how to better approach my next social interaction?

ADHD Medication and
BEHAVIOR Tracker

Week of: ___ / ___ / ___

	M	T	W	T	F	S	S
Initiate Social Contact							
Social Contact Results							
Medication Time & Dose							
Maintained Daily Routine							
Sleep and Rest hours							
Healthy Diet							
Exercise / Activity							

BEHAVIOR TRACKER

	M	T	W	T	F	S	S
Became Irritable	1 — 10	1 — 10	1 — 10	1 — 10	1 — 10	1 — 10	1 — 10
Felt Agitated	1 — 10	1 — 10	1 — 10	1 — 10	1 — 10	1 — 10	1 — 10
Unable to concentrate	1 — 10	1 — 10	1 — 10	1 — 10	1 — 10	1 — 10	1 — 10
Memory Loss	1 — 10	1 — 10	1 — 10	1 — 10	1 — 10	1 — 10	1 — 10
Energy Level	1 — 10	1 — 10	1 — 10	1 — 10	1 — 10	1 — 10	1 — 10
Kept Focus	1 — 10	1 — 10	1 — 10	1 — 10	1 — 10	1 — 10	1 — 10
Able to complete tasks	1 — 10	1 — 10	1 — 10	1 — 10	1 — 10	1 — 10	1 — 10
Motivation level	1 — 10	1 — 10	1 — 10	1 — 10	1 — 10	1 — 10	1 — 10
Healthy appetite	1 — 10	1 — 10	1 — 10	1 — 10	1 — 10	1 — 10	1 — 10
Physical symptoms:							
• Headache	1 — 10	1 — 10	1 — 10	1 — 10	1 — 10	1 — 10	1 — 10
• Lethargy	1 — 10	1 — 10	1 — 10	1 — 10	1 — 10	1 — 10	1 — 10
• Nausea	1 — 10	1 — 10	1 — 10	1 — 10	1 — 10	1 — 10	1 — 10
• Other							
Notes							

REJECTION DYSPHORIA WORKSHEET

Date: _____

Time: _____

Where did the social interaction take place?
What exact words were said and by whom?
Then what exactly happened?

What did I think and how did I feel before I reacted to that?

What words did I use to respond? What was the effect of those words on the other person involved?

What was the outcome of this encounter?

If I felt rejected, how could I have reframed my thoughts to ward off that feeling?

Did I learn anything specific about myself or the other person?
Any ideas how to better approach my next social interaction?

ADHD Medication and
BEHAVIOR Tracker

Week of:

____/____/____

	M	T	W	T	F	S	S
Initiate Social Contact							
Social Contact Results							
Medication Time & Dose							
Maintained Daily Routine							
Sleep and Rest hours							
Healthy Diet							
Exercise / Activity							
BEHAVIOR TRACKER							
Became Irritable	1 — 10	1 — 10	1 — 10	1 — 10	1 — 10	1 — 10	1 — 10
Felt Agitated	1 — 10	1 — 10	1 — 10	1 — 10	1 — 10	1 — 10	1 — 10
Unable to concentrate	1 — 10	1 — 10	1 — 10	1 — 10	1 — 10	1 — 10	1 — 10
Memory Loss	1 — 10	1 — 10	1 — 10	1 — 10	1 — 10	1 — 10	1 — 10
Energy Level	1 — 10	1 — 10	1 — 10	1 — 10	1 — 10	1 — 10	1 — 10
Kept Focus	1 — 10	1 — 10	1 — 10	1 — 10	1 — 10	1 — 10	1 — 10
Able to complete tasks	1 — 10	1 — 10	1 — 10	1 — 10	1 — 10	1 — 10	1 — 10
Motivation level	1 — 10	1 — 10	1 — 10	1 — 10	1 — 10	1 — 10	1 — 10
Healthy appetite	1 — 10	1 — 10	1 — 10	1 — 10	1 — 10	1 — 10	1 — 10
Physical symptoms:							
• Headache	1 — 10	1 — 10	1 — 10	1 — 10	1 — 10	1 — 10	1 — 10
• Lethargy	1 — 10	1 — 10	1 — 10	1 — 10	1 — 10	1 — 10	1 — 10
• Nausea	1 — 10	1 — 10	1 — 10	1 — 10	1 — 10	1 — 10	1 — 10
• Other							
Notes							

REJECTION DYSPHORIA WORKSHEET

Date:

Time:

Where did the social interaction take place?
What exact words were said and by whom?
Then what exactly happened?

What did I think and how did I feel before I reacted to that?

What words did I use to respond? What was the effect of those words on the other person involved?

What was the outcome of this encounter?

If I felt rejected, how could I have reframed my thoughts to ward off that feeling?

Did I learn anything specific about myself or the other person? Any ideas how to better approach my next social interaction?

ADHD Medication and
BEHAVIOR Tracker

	M	T	W	T	F	S	S
Initiate Social Contact							
Social Contact Results							
Medication Time & Dose							
Maintained Daily Routine							
Sleep and Rest hours							
Healthy Diet							
Exercise / Activity							

BEHAVIOR TRACKER

	M	T	W	T	F	S	S
Became Irritable	1 — 10	1 — 10	1 — 10	1 — 10	1 — 10	1 — 10	1 — 10
Felt Agitated	1 — 10	1 — 10	1 — 10	1 — 10	1 — 10	1 — 10	1 — 10
Unable to concentrate	1 — 10	1 — 10	1 — 10	1 — 10	1 — 10	1 — 10	1 — 10
Memory Loss	1 — 10	1 — 10	1 — 10	1 — 10	1 — 10	1 — 10	1 — 10
Energy Level	1 — 10	1 — 10	1 — 10	1 — 10	1 — 10	1 — 10	1 — 10
Kept Focus	1 — 10	1 — 10	1 — 10	1 — 10	1 — 10	1 — 10	1 — 10
Able to complete tasks	1 — 10	1 — 10	1 — 10	1 — 10	1 — 10	1 — 10	1 — 10
Motivation level	1 — 10	1 — 10	1 — 10	1 — 10	1 — 10	1 — 10	1 — 10
Healthy appetite	1 — 10	1 — 10	1 — 10	1 — 10	1 — 10	1 — 10	1 — 10
Physical symptoms:							
• Headache	1 — 10	1 — 10	1 — 10	1 — 10	1 — 10	1 — 10	1 — 10
• Lethargy	1 — 10	1 — 10	1 — 10	1 — 10	1 — 10	1 — 10	1 — 10
• Nausea	1 — 10	1 — 10	1 — 10	1 — 10	1 — 10	1 — 10	1 — 10
• Other							
Notes							

REJECTION DYSPHORIA WORKSHEET

Date: _____

Time: _____

Where did the social interaction take place?
What exact words were said and by whom?
Then what exactly happened?

What did I think and how did I feel before I reacted to that?

What words did I use to respond? What was the effect of those words on the other person involved?

What was the outcome of this encounter?

If I felt rejected, how could I have reframed my thoughts to ward off that feeling?

Did I learn anything specific about myself or the other person? Any ideas how to better approach my next social interaction?

ADHD Medication and
BEHAVIOR Tracker

Week of:

_____/_____/_____

	M	T	W	T	F	S	S
Initiate Social Contact							
Social Contact Results							
Medication Time & Dose							
Maintained Daily Routine							
Sleep and Rest hours							
Healthy Diet							
Exercise / Activity							
BEHAVIOR TRACKER							
Became Irritable	1 — 10	1 — 10	1 — 10	1 — 10	1 — 10	1 — 10	1 — 10
Felt Agitated	1 — 10	1 — 10	1 — 10	1 — 10	1 — 10	1 — 10	1 — 10
Unable to concentrate	1 — 10	1 — 10	1 — 10	1 — 10	1 — 10	1 — 10	1 — 10
Memory Loss	1 — 10	1 — 10	1 — 10	1 — 10	1 — 10	1 — 10	1 — 10
Energy Level	1 — 10	1 — 10	1 — 10	1 — 10	1 — 10	1 — 10	1 — 10
Kept Focus	1 — 10	1 — 10	1 — 10	1 — 10	1 — 10	1 — 10	1 — 10
Able to complete tasks	1 — 10	1 — 10	1 — 10	1 — 10	1 — 10	1 — 10	1 — 10
Motivation level	1 — 10	1 — 10	1 — 10	1 — 10	1 — 10	1 — 10	1 — 10
Healthy appetite	1 — 10	1 — 10	1 — 10	1 — 10	1 — 10	1 — 10	1 — 10
Physical symptoms:							
• Headache	1 — 10	1 — 10	1 — 10	1 — 10	1 — 10	1 — 10	1 — 10
• Lethargy	1 — 10	1 — 10	1 — 10	1 — 10	1 — 10	1 — 10	1 — 10
• Nausea	1 — 10	1 — 10	1 — 10	1 — 10	1 — 10	1 — 10	1 — 10
• Other							
Notes							

REJECTION DYSPHORIA WORKSHEET

Date:
_____

Time:
_____

Where did the social interaction take place?
What exact words were said and by whom?
Then what exactly happened?

What did I think and how did I feel before I reacted to that?

What words did I use to respond?
What was the effect of those words on the other person involved?

What was the outcome of this encounter?

If I felt rejected, how could I have reframed my thoughts to ward off that feeling?

Did I learn anything specific about myself or the other person?
Any ideas how to better approach my next social interaction?

ADHD Medication and
BEHAVIOR Tracker

Week of:

___/___/___

	M	T	W	T	F	S	S
Initiate Social Contact							
Social Contact Results							
Medication Time & Dose							
Maintained Daily Routine							
Sleep and Rest hours							
Healthy Diet							
Exercise / Activity							
BEHAVIOR TRACKER							
Became Irritable	1 — 10	1 — 10	1 — 10	1 — 10	1 — 10	1 — 10	1 — 10
Felt Agitated	1 — 10	1 — 10	1 — 10	1 — 10	1 — 10	1 — 10	1 — 10
Unable to concentrate	1 — 10	1 — 10	1 — 10	1 — 10	1 — 10	1 — 10	1 — 10
Memory Loss	1 — 10	1 — 10	1 — 10	1 — 10	1 — 10	1 — 10	1 — 10
Energy Level	1 — 10	1 — 10	1 — 10	1 — 10	1 — 10	1 — 10	1 — 10
Kept Focus	1 — 10	1 — 10	1 — 10	1 — 10	1 — 10	1 — 10	1 — 10
Able to complete tasks	1 — 10	1 — 10	1 — 10	1 — 10	1 — 10	1 — 10	1 — 10
Motivation level	1 — 10	1 — 10	1 — 10	1 — 10	1 — 10	1 — 10	1 — 10
Healthy appetite	1 — 10	1 — 10	1 — 10	1 — 10	1 — 10	1 — 10	1 — 10
Physical symptoms:							
• Headache	1 — 10	1 — 10	1 — 10	1 — 10	1 — 10	1 — 10	1 — 10
• Lethargy	1 — 10	1 — 10	1 — 10	1 — 10	1 — 10	1 — 10	1 — 10
• Nausea	1 — 10	1 — 10	1 — 10	1 — 10	1 — 10	1 — 10	1 — 10
• Other							
Notes							

REJECTION DYSPHORIA WORKSHEET

Date: _____

Time: _____

Where did the social interaction take place?
What exact words were said and by whom?
Then what exactly happened?

What did I think and how did I feel before I reacted to that?

What words did I use to respond? What was the effect of those words on the other person involved?

What was the outcome of this encounter?

If I felt rejected, how could I have reframed my thoughts to ward off that feeling?

Did I learn anything specific about myself or the other person? Any ideas how to better approach my next social interaction?

ADHD Medication and
BEHAVIOR Tracker

Week of: ____/____/____

	M	T	W	T	F	S	S
Initiate Social Contact							
Social Contact Results							
Medication Time & Dose							
Maintained Daily Routine							
Sleep and Rest hours							
Healthy Diet							
Exercise / Activity							

BEHAVIOR TRACKER

	M	T	W	T	F	S	S
Became Irritable	1 — 10	1 — 10	1 — 10	1 — 10	1 — 10	1 — 10	1 — 10
Felt Agitated	1 — 10	1 — 10	1 — 10	1 — 10	1 — 10	1 — 10	1 — 10
Unable to concentrate	1 — 10	1 — 10	1 — 10	1 — 10	1 — 10	1 — 10	1 — 10
Memory Loss	1 — 10	1 — 10	1 — 10	1 — 10	1 — 10	1 — 10	1 — 10
Energy Level	1 — 10	1 — 10	1 — 10	1 — 10	1 — 10	1 — 10	1 — 10
Kept Focus	1 — 10	1 — 10	1 — 10	1 — 10	1 — 10	1 — 10	1 — 10
Able to complete tasks	1 — 10	1 — 10	1 — 10	1 — 10	1 — 10	1 — 10	1 — 10
Motivation level	1 — 10	1 — 10	1 — 10	1 — 10	1 — 10	1 — 10	1 — 10
Healthy appetite	1 — 10	1 — 10	1 — 10	1 — 10	1 — 10	1 — 10	1 — 10
Physical symptoms:							
• Headache	1 — 10	1 — 10	1 — 10	1 — 10	1 — 10	1 — 10	1 — 10
• Lethargy	1 — 10	1 — 10	1 — 10	1 — 10	1 — 10	1 — 10	1 — 10
• Nausea	1 — 10	1 — 10	1 — 10	1 — 10	1 — 10	1 — 10	1 — 10
• Other							
Notes							

REJECTION DYSPHORIA WORKSHEET

Date:
_____

Time:
_____

Where did the social interaction take place?
What exact words were said and by whom?
Then what exactly happened?

What did I think and how did I feel before I reacted to that?

What words did I use to respond? What was the effect of those words on the other person involved?

What was the outcome of this encounter?

If I felt rejected, how could I have reframed my thoughts to ward off that feeling?

Did I learn anything specific about myself or the other person? Any ideas how to better approach my next social interaction?

ADHD Medication and
BEHAVIOR Tracker

Week of: ____/____/____

	M	T	W	T	F	S	S
Initiate Social Contact							
Social Contact Results							
Medication Time & Dose							
Maintained Daily Routine							
Sleep and Rest hours							
Healthy Diet							
Exercise / Activity							

BEHAVIOR TRACKER

	M	T	W	T	F	S	S
Became Irritable	1 — 10	1 — 10	1 — 10	1 — 10	1 — 10	1 — 10	1 — 10
Felt Agitated	1 — 10	1 — 10	1 — 10	1 — 10	1 — 10	1 — 10	1 — 10
Unable to concentrate	1 — 10	1 — 10	1 — 10	1 — 10	1 — 10	1 — 10	1 — 10
Memory Loss	1 — 10	1 — 10	1 — 10	1 — 10	1 — 10	1 — 10	1 — 10
Energy Level	1 — 10	1 — 10	1 — 10	1 — 10	1 — 10	1 — 10	1 — 10
Kept Focus	1 — 10	1 — 10	1 — 10	1 — 10	1 — 10	1 — 10	1 — 10
Able to complete tasks	1 — 10	1 — 10	1 — 10	1 — 10	1 — 10	1 — 10	1 — 10
Motivation level	1 — 10	1 — 10	1 — 10	1 — 10	1 — 10	1 — 10	1 — 10
Healthy appetite	1 — 10	1 — 10	1 — 10	1 — 10	1 — 10	1 — 10	1 — 10
Physical symptoms:							
• Headache	1 — 10	1 — 10	1 — 10	1 — 10	1 — 10	1 — 10	1 — 10
• Lethargy	1 — 10	1 — 10	1 — 10	1 — 10	1 — 10	1 — 10	1 — 10
• Nausea	1 — 10	1 — 10	1 — 10	1 — 10	1 — 10	1 — 10	1 — 10
• Other							
Notes							

REJECTION DYSPHORIA WORKSHEET

Date: _____

Time: _____

Where did the social interaction take place?
What exact words were said and by whom?
Then what exactly happened?

What did I think and how did I feel before I reacted to that?

What words did I use to respond? What was the effect of those words on the other person involved?

What was the outcome of this encounter?

If I felt rejected, how could I have reframed my thoughts to ward off that feeling?

Did I learn anything specific about myself or the other person? Any ideas how to better approach my next social interaction?

ADHD Medication and
BEHAVIOR Tracker

Week of: ___/___/___

	M	T	W	T	F	S	S
Initiate Social Contact							
Social Contact Results							
Medication Time & Dose							
Maintained Daily Routine							
Sleep and Rest hours							
Healthy Diet							
Exercise / Activity							

BEHAVIOR TRACKER

	M	T	W	T	F	S	S
Became Irritable	1 — 10	1 — 10	1 — 10	1 — 10	1 — 10	1 — 10	1 — 10
Felt Agitated	1 — 10	1 — 10	1 — 10	1 — 10	1 — 10	1 — 10	1 — 10
Unable to concentrate	1 — 10	1 — 10	1 — 10	1 — 10	1 — 10	1 — 10	1 — 10
Memory Loss	1 — 10	1 — 10	1 — 10	1 — 10	1 — 10	1 — 10	1 — 10
Energy Level	1 — 10	1 — 10	1 — 10	1 — 10	1 — 10	1 — 10	1 — 10
Kept Focus	1 — 10	1 — 10	1 — 10	1 — 10	1 — 10	1 — 10	1 — 10
Able to complete tasks	1 — 10	1 — 10	1 — 10	1 — 10	1 — 10	1 — 10	1 — 10
Motivation level	1 — 10	1 — 10	1 — 10	1 — 10	1 — 10	1 — 10	1 — 10
Healthy appetite	1 — 10	1 — 10	1 — 10	1 — 10	1 — 10	1 — 10	1 — 10
Physical symptoms:							
• Headache	1 — 10	1 — 10	1 — 10	1 — 10	1 — 10	1 — 10	1 — 10
• Lethargy	1 — 10	1 — 10	1 — 10	1 — 10	1 — 10	1 — 10	1 — 10
• Nausea	1 — 10	1 — 10	1 — 10	1 — 10	1 — 10	1 — 10	1 — 10
• Other							
Notes							

REJECTION DYSPHORIA WORKSHEET

Date: _____

Time: _____

Where did the social interaction take place?
What exact words were said and by whom?
Then what exactly happened?

What did I think and how did I feel before I reacted to that?

What words did I use to respond? What was the effect of those words on the other person involved?

What was the outcome of this encounter?

If I felt rejected, how could I have reframed my thoughts to ward off that feeling?

Did I learn anything specific about myself or the other person? Any ideas how to better approach my next social interaction?

ADHD Medication and
BEHAVIOR Tracker

Week of: _____/_____/_____

	M	T	W	T	F	S	S
Initiate Social Contact							
Social Contact Results							
Medication Time & Dose							
Maintained Daily Routine							
Sleep and Rest hours							
Healthy Diet							
Exercise / Activity							

BEHAVIOR TRACKER

	M	T	W	T	F	S	S
Became Irritable	1 — 10	1 — 10	1 — 10	1 — 10	1 — 10	1 — 10	1 — 10
Felt Agitated	1 — 10	1 — 10	1 — 10	1 — 10	1 — 10	1 — 10	1 — 10
Unable to concentrate	1 — 10	1 — 10	1 — 10	1 — 10	1 — 10	1 — 10	1 — 10
Memory Loss	1 — 10	1 — 10	1 — 10	1 — 10	1 — 10	1 — 10	1 — 10
Energy Level	1 — 10	1 — 10	1 — 10	1 — 10	1 — 10	1 — 10	1 — 10
Kept Focus	1 — 10	1 — 10	1 — 10	1 — 10	1 — 10	1 — 10	1 — 10
Able to complete tasks	1 — 10	1 — 10	1 — 10	1 — 10	1 — 10	1 — 10	1 — 10
Motivation level	1 — 10	1 — 10	1 — 10	1 — 10	1 — 10	1 — 10	1 — 10
Healthy appetite	1 — 10	1 — 10	1 — 10	1 — 10	1 — 10	1 — 10	1 — 10
Physical symptoms:							
• Headache	1 — 10	1 — 10	1 — 10	1 — 10	1 — 10	1 — 10	1 — 10
• Lethargy	1 — 10	1 — 10	1 — 10	1 — 10	1 — 10	1 — 10	1 — 10
• Nausea	1 — 10	1 — 10	1 — 10	1 — 10	1 — 10	1 — 10	1 — 10
• Other							
Notes							

REJECTION DYSPHORIA WORKSHEET

Date:
_____

Time:
_____

Where did the social interaction take place?
What exact words were said and by whom?
Then what exactly happened?

What did I think and how did I feel before I reacted to that?

What words did I use to respond?
What was the effect of those words on the other person involved?

What was the outcome of this encounter?

If I felt rejected, how could I have reframed my thoughts to ward off that feeling?

Did I learn anything specific about myself or the other person?
Any ideas how to better approach my next social interaction?

ADHD Medication and
BEHAVIOR Tracker

Week of: ____/____/____

	M	T	W	T	F	S	S
Initiate Social Contact							
Social Contact Results							
Medication Time & Dose							
Maintained Daily Routine							
Sleep and Rest hours							
Healthy Diet							
Exercise / Activity							
BEHAVIOR TRACKER							
Became Irritable	1 — 10	1 — 10	1 — 10	1 — 10	1 — 10	1 — 10	1 — 10
Felt Agitated	1 — 10	1 — 10	1 — 10	1 — 10	1 — 10	1 — 10	1 — 10
Unable to concentrate	1 — 10	1 — 10	1 — 10	1 — 10	1 — 10	1 — 10	1 — 10
Memory Loss	1 — 10	1 — 10	1 — 10	1 — 10	1 — 10	1 — 10	1 — 10
Energy Level	1 — 10	1 — 10	1 — 10	1 — 10	1 — 10	1 — 10	1 — 10
Kept Focus	1 — 10	1 — 10	1 — 10	1 — 10	1 — 10	1 — 10	1 — 10
Able to complete tasks	1 — 10	1 — 10	1 — 10	1 — 10	1 — 10	1 — 10	1 — 10
Motivation level	1 — 10	1 — 10	1 — 10	1 — 10	1 — 10	1 — 10	1 — 10
Healthy appetite	1 — 10	1 — 10	1 — 10	1 — 10	1 — 10	1 — 10	1 — 10
Physical symptoms:							
• Headache	1 — 10	1 — 10	1 — 10	1 — 10	1 — 10	1 — 10	1 — 10
• Lethargy	1 — 10	1 — 10	1 — 10	1 — 10	1 — 10	1 — 10	1 — 10
• Nausea	1 — 10	1 — 10	1 — 10	1 — 10	1 — 10	1 — 10	1 — 10
• Other							
Notes							

REJECTION DYSPHORIA WORKSHEET

Date: _____

Time: _____

Where did the social interaction take place?
What exact words were said and by whom?
Then what exactly happened?

What did I think and how did I feel before I reacted to that?

What words did I use to respond? What was the effect of those words on the other person involved?

What was the outcome of this encounter?

If I felt rejected, how could I have reframed my thoughts to ward off that feeling?

Did I learn anything specific about myself or the other person?
Any ideas how to better approach my next social interaction?

ADHD Medication and
BEHAVIOR Tracker

Week of:

_____/_____/_____

	M	T	W	T	F	S	S
Initiate Social Contact							
Social Contact Results							
Medication Time & Dose							
Maintained Daily Routine							
Sleep and Rest hours							
Healthy Diet							
Exercise / Activity							

BEHAVIOR TRACKER

	M	T	W	T	F	S	S
Became Irritable	1 — 10	1 — 10	1 — 10	1 — 10	1 — 10	1 — 10	1 — 10
Felt Agitated	1 — 10	1 — 10	1 — 10	1 — 10	1 — 10	1 — 10	1 — 10
Unable to concentrate	1 — 10	1 — 10	1 — 10	1 — 10	1 — 10	1 — 10	1 — 10
Memory Loss	1 — 10	1 — 10	1 — 10	1 — 10	1 — 10	1 — 10	1 — 10
Energy Level	1 — 10	1 — 10	1 — 10	1 — 10	1 — 10	1 — 10	1 — 10
Kept Focus	1 — 10	1 — 10	1 — 10	1 — 10	1 — 10	1 — 10	1 — 10
Able to complete tasks	1 — 10	1 — 10	1 — 10	1 — 10	1 — 10	1 — 10	1 — 10
Motivation level	1 — 10	1 — 10	1 — 10	1 — 10	1 — 10	1 — 10	1 — 10
Healthy appetite	1 — 10	1 — 10	1 — 10	1 — 10	1 — 10	1 — 10	1 — 10
Physical symptoms:							
• Headache	1 — 10	1 — 10	1 — 10	1 — 10	1 — 10	1 — 10	1 — 10
• Lethargy	1 — 10	1 — 10	1 — 10	1 — 10	1 — 10	1 — 10	1 — 10
• Nausea	1 — 10	1 — 10	1 — 10	1 — 10	1 — 10	1 — 10	1 — 10
• Other							
Notes							

REJECTION DYSPHORIA WORKSHEET

Date: _____

Time: _____

Where did the social interaction take place?
What exact words were said and by whom?
Then what exactly happened?

What did I think and how did I feel before I reacted to that?

What words did I use to respond? What was the effect of those words on the other person involved?

What was the outcome of this encounter?

If I felt rejected, how could I have reframed my thoughts to ward off that feeling?

Did I learn anything specific about myself or the other person? Any ideas how to better approach my next social interaction?

ADHD Medication and
BEHAVIOR Tracker

Week of: ____ / ____ / ____

	M	T	W	T	F	S	S
Initiate Social Contact							
Social Contact Results							
Medication Time & Dose							
Maintained Daily Routine							
Sleep and Rest hours							
Healthy Diet							
Exercise / Activity							

BEHAVIOR TRACKER

	M	T	W	T	F	S	S
Became Irritable	1 — 10	1 — 10	1 — 10	1 — 10	1 — 10	1 — 10	1 — 10
Felt Agitated	1 — 10	1 — 10	1 — 10	1 — 10	1 — 10	1 — 10	1 — 10
Unable to concentrate	1 — 10	1 — 10	1 — 10	1 — 10	1 — 10	1 — 10	1 — 10
Memory Loss	1 — 10	1 — 10	1 — 10	1 — 10	1 — 10	1 — 10	1 — 10
Energy Level	1 — 10	1 — 10	1 — 10	1 — 10	1 — 10	1 — 10	1 — 10
Kept Focus	1 — 10	1 — 10	1 — 10	1 — 10	1 — 10	1 — 10	1 — 10
Able to complete tasks	1 — 10	1 — 10	1 — 10	1 — 10	1 — 10	1 — 10	1 — 10
Motivation level	1 — 10	1 — 10	1 — 10	1 — 10	1 — 10	1 — 10	1 — 10
Healthy appetite	1 — 10	1 — 10	1 — 10	1 — 10	1 — 10	1 — 10	1 — 10
Physical symptoms:							
• Headache	1 — 10	1 — 10	1 — 10	1 — 10	1 — 10	1 — 10	1 — 10
• Lethargy	1 — 10	1 — 10	1 — 10	1 — 10	1 — 10	1 — 10	1 — 10
• Nausea	1 — 10	1 — 10	1 — 10	1 — 10	1 — 10	1 — 10	1 — 10
• Other							
Notes							

REJECTION DYSPHORIA WORKSHEET

Date: _____

Time: _____

Where did the social interaction take place?
What exact words were said and by whom?
Then what exactly happened?

What did I think and how did I feel before I reacted to that?

What words did I use to respond? What was the effect of those words on the other person involved?

What was the outcome of this encounter?

If I felt rejected, how could I have reframed my thoughts to ward off that feeling?

Did I learn anything specific about myself or the other person? Any ideas how to better approach my next social interaction?

ADHD Medication and
BEHAVIOR Tracker

Week of:
____/____/____

	M	T	W	T	F	S	S
Initiate Social Contact							
Social Contact Results							
Medication Time & Dose							
Maintained Daily Routine							
Sleep and Rest hours							
Healthy Diet							
Exercise / Activity							
BEHAVIOR TRACKER							
Became Irritable	1 — 10	1 — 10	1 — 10	1 — 10	1 — 10	1 — 10	1 — 10
Felt Agitated	1 — 10	1 — 10	1 — 10	1 — 10	1 — 10	1 — 10	1 — 10
Unable to concentrate	1 — 10	1 — 10	1 — 10	1 — 10	1 — 10	1 — 10	1 — 10
Memory Loss	1 — 10	1 — 10	1 — 10	1 — 10	1 — 10	1 — 10	1 — 10
Energy Level	1 — 10	1 — 10	1 — 10	1 — 10	1 — 10	1 — 10	1 — 10
Kept Focus	1 — 10	1 — 10	1 — 10	1 — 10	1 — 10	1 — 10	1 — 10
Able to complete tasks	1 — 10	1 — 10	1 — 10	1 — 10	1 — 10	1 — 10	1 — 10
Motivation level	1 — 10	1 — 10	1 — 10	1 — 10	1 — 10	1 — 10	1 — 10
Healthy appetite	1 — 10	1 — 10	1 — 10	1 — 10	1 — 10	1 — 10	1 — 10
Physical symptoms:							
• Headache	1 — 10	1 — 10	1 — 10	1 — 10	1 — 10	1 — 10	1 — 10
• Lethargy	1 — 10	1 — 10	1 — 10	1 — 10	1 — 10	1 — 10	1 — 10
• Nausea	1 — 10	1 — 10	1 — 10	1 — 10	1 — 10	1 — 10	1 — 10
• Other							
Notes							

REJECTION DYSPHORIA WORKSHEET

Date:
_____

Time:
_____

Where did the social interaction take place?
What exact words were said and by whom?
Then what exactly happened?

What did I think and how did I feel before I reacted to that?

What words did I use to respond? What was the effect of those words on the other person involved?

What was the outcome of this encounter?

If I felt rejected, how could I have reframed my thoughts to ward off that feeling?

Did I learn anything specific about myself or the other person? Any ideas how to better approach my next social interaction?

ADHD Medication and
BEHAVIOR Tracker

Week of:

____/____/____

	M	T	W	T	F	S	S
Initiate Social Contact							
Social Contact Results							
Medication Time & Dose							
Maintained Daily Routine							
Sleep and Rest hours							
Healthy Diet							
Exercise / Activity							

BEHAVIOR TRACKER

	M	T	W	T	F	S	S
Became Irritable	1 — 10	1 — 10	1 — 10	1 — 10	1 — 10	1 — 10	1 — 10
Felt Agitated	1 — 10	1 — 10	1 — 10	1 — 10	1 — 10	1 — 10	1 — 10
Unable to concentrate	1 — 10	1 — 10	1 — 10	1 — 10	1 — 10	1 — 10	1 — 10
Memory Loss	1 — 10	1 — 10	1 — 10	1 — 10	1 — 10	1 — 10	1 — 10
Energy Level	1 — 10	1 — 10	1 — 10	1 — 10	1 — 10	1 — 10	1 — 10
Kept Focus	1 — 10	1 — 10	1 — 10	1 — 10	1 — 10	1 — 10	1 — 10
Able to complete tasks	1 — 10	1 — 10	1 — 10	1 — 10	1 — 10	1 — 10	1 — 10
Motivation level	1 — 10	1 — 10	1 — 10	1 — 10	1 — 10	1 — 10	1 — 10
Healthy appetite	1 — 10	1 — 10	1 — 10	1 — 10	1 — 10	1 — 10	1 — 10
Physical symptoms:							
• Headache	1 — 10	1 — 10	1 — 10	1 — 10	1 — 10	1 — 10	1 — 10
• Lethargy	1 — 10	1 — 10	1 — 10	1 — 10	1 — 10	1 — 10	1 — 10
• Nausea	1 — 10	1 — 10	1 — 10	1 — 10	1 — 10	1 — 10	1 — 10
• Other							
Notes							

REJECTION DYSPHORIA WORKSHEET

Date: _____

Time: _____

Where did the social interaction take place?
What exact words were said and by whom?
Then what exactly happened?

What did I think and how did I feel before I reacted to that?

What words did I use to respond? What was the effect of those words on the other person involved?

What was the outcome of this encounter?

If I felt rejected, how could I have reframed my thoughts to ward off that feeling?

Did I learn anything specific about myself or the other person? Any ideas how to better approach my next social interaction?

ADHD Medication and
BEHAVIOR Tracker

Week of:

___/___/___

	M	T	W	T	F	S	S
Initiate Social Contact							
Social Contact Results							
Medication Time & Dose							
Maintained Daily Routine							
Sleep and Rest hours							
Healthy Diet							
Exercise / Activity							
BEHAVIOR TRACKER							
Became Irritable	1 — 10	1 — 10	1 — 10	1 — 10	1 — 10	1 — 10	1 — 10
Felt Agitated	1 — 10	1 — 10	1 — 10	1 — 10	1 — 10	1 — 10	1 — 10
Unable to concentrate	1 — 10	1 — 10	1 — 10	1 — 10	1 — 10	1 — 10	1 — 10
Memory Loss	1 — 10	1 — 10	1 — 10	1 — 10	1 — 10	1 — 10	1 — 10
Energy Level	1 — 10	1 — 10	1 — 10	1 — 10	1 — 10	1 — 10	1 — 10
Kept Focus	1 — 10	1 — 10	1 — 10	1 — 10	1 — 10	1 — 10	1 — 10
Able to complete tasks	1 — 10	1 — 10	1 — 10	1 — 10	1 — 10	1 — 10	1 — 10
Motivation level	1 — 10	1 — 10	1 — 10	1 — 10	1 — 10	1 — 10	1 — 10
Healthy appetite	1 — 10	1 — 10	1 — 10	1 — 10	1 — 10	1 — 10	1 — 10
Physical symptoms:							
• Headache	1 — 10	1 — 10	1 — 10	1 — 10	1 — 10	1 — 10	1 — 10
• Lethargy	1 — 10	1 — 10	1 — 10	1 — 10	1 — 10	1 — 10	1 — 10
• Nausea	1 — 10	1 — 10	1 — 10	1 — 10	1 — 10	1 — 10	1 — 10
• Other							
Notes							

REJECTION DYSPHORIA WORKSHEET

Date:

_____

Time:

_____

Where did the social interaction take place?
What exact words were said and by whom?
Then what exactly happened?

What did I think and how did I feel before I reacted to that?

What words did I use to respond? What was the effect of those words on the other person involved?

What was the outcome of this encounter?

If I felt rejected, how could I have reframed my thoughts to ward off that feeling?

Did I learn anything specific about myself or the other person?
Any ideas how to better approach my next social interaction?

ADHD Medication and
BEHAVIOR Tracker

Week of: ____/____/____

	M	T	W	T	F	S	S
Initiate Social Contact							
Social Contact Results							
Medication Time & Dose							
Maintained Daily Routine							
Sleep and Rest hours							
Healthy Diet							
Exercise / Activity							

BEHAVIOR TRACKER

	M	T	W	T	F	S	S
Became Irritable	1 — 10	1 — 10	1 — 10	1 — 10	1 — 10	1 — 10	1 — 10
Felt Agitated	1 — 10	1 — 10	1 — 10	1 — 10	1 — 10	1 — 10	1 — 10
Unable to concentrate	1 — 10	1 — 10	1 — 10	1 — 10	1 — 10	1 — 10	1 — 10
Memory Loss	1 — 10	1 — 10	1 — 10	1 — 10	1 — 10	1 — 10	1 — 10
Energy Level	1 — 10	1 — 10	1 — 10	1 — 10	1 — 10	1 — 10	1 — 10
Kept Focus	1 — 10	1 — 10	1 — 10	1 — 10	1 — 10	1 — 10	1 — 10
Able to complete tasks	1 — 10	1 — 10	1 — 10	1 — 10	1 — 10	1 — 10	1 — 10
Motivation level	1 — 10	1 — 10	1 — 10	1 — 10	1 — 10	1 — 10	1 — 10
Healthy appetite	1 — 10	1 — 10	1 — 10	1 — 10	1 — 10	1 — 10	1 — 10
Physical symptoms:							
• Headache	1 — 10	1 — 10	1 — 10	1 — 10	1 — 10	1 — 10	1 — 10
• Lethargy	1 — 10	1 — 10	1 — 10	1 — 10	1 — 10	1 — 10	1 — 10
• Nausea	1 — 10	1 — 10	1 — 10	1 — 10	1 — 10	1 — 10	1 — 10
• Other							
Notes							

REJECTION DYSPHORIA WORKSHEET

Date: _____

Time: _____

Where did the social interaction take place?
What exact words were said and by whom?
Then what exactly happened?

What did I think and how did I feel before I reacted to that?

What words did I use to respond? What was the effect of those words on the other person involved?

What was the outcome of this encounter?

If I felt rejected, how could I have reframed my thoughts to ward off that feeling?

Did I learn anything specific about myself or the other person?
Any ideas how to better approach my next social interaction?

ADHD Medication and
BEHAVIOR Tracker

Week of:

___/___/___

	M	T	W	T	F	S	S
Initiate Social Contact							
Social Contact Results							
Medication Time & Dose							
Maintained Daily Routine							
Sleep and Rest hours							
Healthy Diet							
Exercise / Activity							

BEHAVIOR TRACKER

	M	T	W	T	F	S	S
Became Irritable	1 — 10	1 — 10	1 — 10	1 — 10	1 — 10	1 — 10	1 — 10
Felt Agitated	1 — 10	1 — 10	1 — 10	1 — 10	1 — 10	1 — 10	1 — 10
Unable to concentrate	1 — 10	1 — 10	1 — 10	1 — 10	1 — 10	1 — 10	1 — 10
Memory Loss	1 — 10	1 — 10	1 — 10	1 — 10	1 — 10	1 — 10	1 — 10
Energy Level	1 — 10	1 — 10	1 — 10	1 — 10	1 — 10	1 — 10	1 — 10
Kept Focus	1 — 10	1 — 10	1 — 10	1 — 10	1 — 10	1 — 10	1 — 10
Able to complete tasks	1 — 10	1 — 10	1 — 10	1 — 10	1 — 10	1 — 10	1 — 10
Motivation level	1 — 10	1 — 10	1 — 10	1 — 10	1 — 10	1 — 10	1 — 10
Healthy appetite	1 — 10	1 — 10	1 — 10	1 — 10	1 — 10	1 — 10	1 — 10
Physical symptoms:							
• Headache	1 — 10	1 — 10	1 — 10	1 — 10	1 — 10	1 — 10	1 — 10
• Lethargy	1 — 10	1 — 10	1 — 10	1 — 10	1 — 10	1 — 10	1 — 10
• Nausea	1 — 10	1 — 10	1 — 10	1 — 10	1 — 10	1 — 10	1 — 10
• Other							
Notes							

REJECTION DYSPHORIA WORKSHEET

Date:

Time:

Where did the social interaction take place?
What exact words were said and by whom?
Then what exactly happened?

What did I think and how did I feel before I reacted to that?

What words did I use to respond? What was the effect of those words on the other person involved?

What was the outcome of this encounter?

If I felt rejected, how could I have reframed my thoughts to ward off that feeling?

Did I learn anything specific about myself or the other person? Any ideas how to better approach my next social interaction?

ADHD Medication and
BEHAVIOR Tracker

	M	T	W	T	F	S	S
Initiate Social Contact							
Social Contact Results							
Medication Time & Dose							
Maintained Daily Routine							
Sleep and Rest hours							
Healthy Diet							
Exercise / Activity							
BEHAVIOR TRACKER							
Became Irritable	1 —— 10	1 —— 10	1 —— 10	1 —— 10	1 —— 10	1 —— 10	1 —— 10
Felt Agitated	1 —— 10	1 —— 10	1 —— 10	1 —— 10	1 —— 10	1 —— 10	1 —— 10
Unable to concentrate	1 —— 10	1 —— 10	1 —— 10	1 —— 10	1 —— 10	1 —— 10	1 —— 10
Memory Loss	1 —— 10	1 —— 10	1 —— 10	1 —— 10	1 —— 10	1 —— 10	1 —— 10
Energy Level	1 —— 10	1 —— 10	1 —— 10	1 —— 10	1 —— 10	1 —— 10	1 —— 10
Kept Focus	1 —— 10	1 —— 10	1 —— 10	1 —— 10	1 —— 10	1 —— 10	1 —— 10
Able to complete tasks	1 —— 10	1 —— 10	1 —— 10	1 —— 10	1 —— 10	1 —— 10	1 —— 10
Motivation level	1 —— 10	1 —— 10	1 —— 10	1 —— 10	1 —— 10	1 —— 10	1 —— 10
Healthy appetite	1 —— 10	1 —— 10	1 —— 10	1 —— 10	1 —— 10	1 —— 10	1 —— 10
Physical symptoms:							
• Headache	1 —— 10	1 —— 10	1 —— 10	1 —— 10	1 —— 10	1 —— 10	1 —— 10
• Lethargy	1 —— 10	1 —— 10	1 —— 10	1 —— 10	1 —— 10	1 —— 10	1 —— 10
• Nausea	1 —— 10	1 —— 10	1 —— 10	1 —— 10	1 —— 10	1 —— 10	1 —— 10
• Other							
Notes							

REJECTION DYSPHORIA WORKSHEET

Date: _____

Time: _____

Where did the social interaction take place?
What exact words were said and by whom?
Then what exactly happened?

What did I think and how did I feel before I reacted to that?

What words did I use to respond? What was the effect of those words on the other person involved?

What was the outcome of this encounter?

If I felt rejected, how could I have reframed my thoughts to ward off that feeling?

Did I learn anything specific about myself or the other person? Any ideas how to better approach my next social interaction?

ADHD Medication and
BEHAVIOR Tracker

Week of: ____/____/____

	M	T	W	T	F	S	S
Initiate Social Contact							
Social Contact Results							
Medication Time & Dose							
Maintained Daily Routine							
Sleep and Rest hours							
Healthy Diet							
Exercise / Activity							

BEHAVIOR TRACKER

	M	T	W	T	F	S	S
Became Irritable	1—10	1—10	1—10	1—10	1—10	1—10	1—10
Felt Agitated	1—10	1—10	1—10	1—10	1—10	1—10	1—10
Unable to concentrate	1—10	1—10	1—10	1—10	1—10	1—10	1—10
Memory Loss	1—10	1—10	1—10	1—10	1—10	1—10	1—10
Energy Level	1—10	1—10	1—10	1—10	1—10	1—10	1—10
Kept Focus	1—10	1—10	1—10	1—10	1—10	1—10	1—10
Able to complete tasks	1—10	1—10	1—10	1—10	1—10	1—10	1—10
Motivation level	1—10	1—10	1—10	1—10	1—10	1—10	1—10
Healthy appetite	1—10	1—10	1—10	1—10	1—10	1—10	1—10
Physical symptoms:							
• Headache	1—10	1—10	1—10	1—10	1—10	1—10	1—10
• Lethargy	1—10	1—10	1—10	1—10	1—10	1—10	1—10
• Nausea	1—10	1—10	1—10	1—10	1—10	1—10	1—10
• Other							
Notes							

REJECTION DYSPHORIA WORKSHEET

Date: _____

Time: _____

Where did the social interaction take place?
What exact words were said and by whom?
Then what exactly happened?

What did I think and how did I feel before I reacted to that?

What words did I use to respond? What was the effect of those words on the other person involved?

What was the outcome of this encounter?

If I felt rejected, how could I have reframed my thoughts to ward off that feeling?

Did I learn anything specific about myself or the other person? Any ideas how to better approach my next social interaction?

ADHD Medication and
BEHAVIOR Tracker

Week of:

____/____/____

	M	T	W	T	F	S	S
Initiate Social Contact							
Social Contact Results							
Medication Time & Dose							
Maintained Daily Routine							
Sleep and Rest hours							
Healthy Diet							
Exercise / Activity							

BEHAVIOR TRACKER

	M	T	W	T	F	S	S
Became Irritable	1 — 10	1 — 10	1 — 10	1 — 10	1 — 10	1 — 10	1 — 10
Felt Agitated	1 — 10	1 — 10	1 — 10	1 — 10	1 — 10	1 — 10	1 — 10
Unable to concentrate	1 — 10	1 — 10	1 — 10	1 — 10	1 — 10	1 — 10	1 — 10
Memory Loss	1 — 10	1 — 10	1 — 10	1 — 10	1 — 10	1 — 10	1 — 10
Energy Level	1 — 10	1 — 10	1 — 10	1 — 10	1 — 10	1 — 10	1 — 10
Kept Focus	1 — 10	1 — 10	1 — 10	1 — 10	1 — 10	1 — 10	1 — 10
Able to complete tasks	1 — 10	1 — 10	1 — 10	1 — 10	1 — 10	1 — 10	1 — 10
Motivation level	1 — 10	1 — 10	1 — 10	1 — 10	1 — 10	1 — 10	1 — 10
Healthy appetite	1 — 10	1 — 10	1 — 10	1 — 10	1 — 10	1 — 10	1 — 10
Physical symptoms:							
• Headache	1 — 10	1 — 10	1 — 10	1 — 10	1 — 10	1 — 10	1 — 10
• Lethargy	1 — 10	1 — 10	1 — 10	1 — 10	1 — 10	1 — 10	1 — 10
• Nausea	1 — 10	1 — 10	1 — 10	1 — 10	1 — 10	1 — 10	1 — 10
• Other							
Notes							

REJECTION DYSPHORIA WORKSHEET

Date: _____

Time: _____

Where did the social interaction take place?
What exact words were said and by whom?
Then what exactly happened?

What did I think and how did I feel before I reacted to that?

What words did I use to respond? What was the effect of those words on the other person involved?

What was the outcome of this encounter?

If I felt rejected, how could I have reframed my thoughts to ward off that feeling?

Did I learn anything specific about myself or the other person? Any ideas how to better approach my next social interaction?

ADHD Medication and
BEHAVIOR Tracker

Week of:

____/____/____

	M	T	W	T	F	S	S
Initiate Social Contact							
Social Contact Results							
Medication Time & Dose							
Maintained Daily Routine							
Sleep and Rest hours							
Healthy Diet							
Exercise / Activity							
BEHAVIOR TRACKER							
Became Irritable	1 ———— 10	1 ———— 10	1 ———— 10	1 ———— 10	1 ———— 10	1 ———— 10	1 ———— 10
Felt Agitated	1 ———— 10	1 ———— 10	1 ———— 10	1 ———— 10	1 ———— 10	1 ———— 10	1 ———— 10
Unable to concentrate	1 ———— 10	1 ———— 10	1 ———— 10	1 ———— 10	1 ———— 10	1 ———— 10	1 ———— 10
Memory Loss	1 ———— 10	1 ———— 10	1 ———— 10	1 ———— 10	1 ———— 10	1 ———— 10	1 ———— 10
Energy Level	1 ———— 10	1 ———— 10	1 ———— 10	1 ———— 10	1 ———— 10	1 ———— 10	1 ———— 10
Kept Focus	1 ———— 10	1 ———— 10	1 ———— 10	1 ———— 10	1 ———— 10	1 ———— 10	1 ———— 10
Able to complete tasks	1 ———— 10	1 ———— 10	1 ———— 10	1 ———— 10	1 ———— 10	1 ———— 10	1 ———— 10
Motivation level	1 ———— 10	1 ———— 10	1 ———— 10	1 ———— 10	1 ———— 10	1 ———— 10	1 ———— 10
Healthy appetite	1 ———— 10	1 ———— 10	1 ———— 10	1 ———— 10	1 ———— 10	1 ———— 10	1 ———— 10
Physical symptoms:							
• Headache	1 ———— 10	1 ———— 10	1 ———— 10	1 ———— 10	1 ———— 10	1 ———— 10	1 ———— 10
• Lethargy	1 ———— 10	1 ———— 10	1 ———— 10	1 ———— 10	1 ———— 10	1 ———— 10	1 ———— 10
• Nausea	1 ———— 10	1 ———— 10	1 ———— 10	1 ———— 10	1 ———— 10	1 ———— 10	1 ———— 10
• Other							
Notes							

REJECTION DYSPHORIA WORKSHEET

Date: _____

Time: _____

Where did the social interaction take place?
What exact words were said and by whom?
Then what exactly happened?

What did I think and how did I feel before I reacted to that?

What words did I use to respond? What was the effect of those words on the other person involved?

What was the outcome of this encounter?

If I felt rejected, how could I have reframed my thoughts to ward off that feeling?

Did I learn anything specific about myself or the other person? Any ideas how to better approach my next social interaction?

ADHD Medication and
BEHAVIOR Tracker

Week of: ____/____/____

	M	T	W	T	F	S	S
Initiate Social Contact							
Social Contact Results							
Medication Time & Dose							
Maintained Daily Routine							
Sleep and Rest hours							
Healthy Diet							
Exercise / Activity							
BEHAVIOR TRACKER							
Became Irritable	1 — 10	1 — 10	1 — 10	1 — 10	1 — 10	1 — 10	1 — 10
Felt Agitated	1 — 10	1 — 10	1 — 10	1 — 10	1 — 10	1 — 10	1 — 10
Unable to concentrate	1 — 10	1 — 10	1 — 10	1 — 10	1 — 10	1 — 10	1 — 10
Memory Loss	1 — 10	1 — 10	1 — 10	1 — 10	1 — 10	1 — 10	1 — 10
Energy Level	1 — 10	1 — 10	1 — 10	1 — 10	1 — 10	1 — 10	1 — 10
Kept Focus	1 — 10	1 — 10	1 — 10	1 — 10	1 — 10	1 — 10	1 — 10
Able to complete tasks	1 — 10	1 — 10	1 — 10	1 — 10	1 — 10	1 — 10	1 — 10
Motivation level	1 — 10	1 — 10	1 — 10	1 — 10	1 — 10	1 — 10	1 — 10
Healthy appetite	1 — 10	1 — 10	1 — 10	1 — 10	1 — 10	1 — 10	1 — 10
Physical symptoms:							
• Headache	1 — 10	1 — 10	1 — 10	1 — 10	1 — 10	1 — 10	1 — 10
• Lethargy	1 — 10	1 — 10	1 — 10	1 — 10	1 — 10	1 — 10	1 — 10
• Nausea	1 — 10	1 — 10	1 — 10	1 — 10	1 — 10	1 — 10	1 — 10
• Other							
Notes							

REJECTION DYSPHORIA WORKSHEET

Date: _____

Time: _____

Where did the social interaction take place?
What exact words were said and by whom?
Then what exactly happened?

What did I think and how did I feel before I reacted to that?

What words did I use to respond? What was the effect of those words on the other person involved?

What was the outcome of this encounter?

If I felt rejected, how could I have reframed my thoughts to ward off that feeling?

Did I learn anything specific about myself or the other person?
Any ideas how to better approach my next social interaction?

ADHD Medication and
BEHAVIOR Tracker

Week of:

_____ / _____ / _____

	M	T	W	T	F	S	S
Initiate Social Contact							
Social Contact Results							
Medication Time & Dose							
Maintained Daily Routine							
Sleep and Rest hours							
Healthy Diet							
Exercise / Activity							
BEHAVIOR TRACKER							
Became Irritable	1 — 10	1 — 10	1 — 10	1 — 10	1 — 10	1 — 10	1 — 10
Felt Agitated	1 — 10	1 — 10	1 — 10	1 — 10	1 — 10	1 — 10	1 — 10
Unable to concentrate	1 — 10	1 — 10	1 — 10	1 — 10	1 — 10	1 — 10	1 — 10
Memory Loss	1 — 10	1 — 10	1 — 10	1 — 10	1 — 10	1 — 10	1 — 10
Energy Level	1 — 10	1 — 10	1 — 10	1 — 10	1 — 10	1 — 10	1 — 10
Kept Focus	1 — 10	1 — 10	1 — 10	1 — 10	1 — 10	1 — 10	1 — 10
Able to complete tasks	1 — 10	1 — 10	1 — 10	1 — 10	1 — 10	1 — 10	1 — 10
Motivation level	1 — 10	1 — 10	1 — 10	1 — 10	1 — 10	1 — 10	1 — 10
Healthy appetite	1 — 10	1 — 10	1 — 10	1 — 10	1 — 10	1 — 10	1 — 10
Physical symptoms:							
• Headache	1 — 10	1 — 10	1 — 10	1 — 10	1 — 10	1 — 10	1 — 10
• Lethargy	1 — 10	1 — 10	1 — 10	1 — 10	1 — 10	1 — 10	1 — 10
• Nausea	1 — 10	1 — 10	1 — 10	1 — 10	1 — 10	1 — 10	1 — 10
• Other							
Notes							

REJECTION DYSPHORIA WORKSHEET

Date: _____

Time: _____

Where did the social interaction take place?
What exact words were said and by whom?
Then what exactly happened?

What did I think and how did I feel before I reacted to that?

What words did I use to respond? What was the effect of those words on the other person involved?

What was the outcome of this encounter?

If I felt rejected, how could I have reframed my thoughts to ward off that feeling?

Did I learn anything specific about myself or the other person? Any ideas how to better approach my next social interaction?

ADHD Medication and
BEHAVIOR Tracker

	M	T	W	T	F	S	S
Initiate Social Contact							
Social Contact Results							
Medication Time & Dose							
Maintained Daily Routine							
Sleep and Rest hours							
Healthy Diet							
Exercise / Activity							

BEHAVIOR TRACKER

	M	T	W	T	F	S	S
Became Irritable	1 — 10	1 — 10	1 — 10	1 — 10	1 — 10	1 — 10	1 — 10
Felt Agitated	1 — 10	1 — 10	1 — 10	1 — 10	1 — 10	1 — 10	1 — 10
Unable to concentrate	1 — 10	1 — 10	1 — 10	1 — 10	1 — 10	1 — 10	1 — 10
Memory Loss	1 — 10	1 — 10	1 — 10	1 — 10	1 — 10	1 — 10	1 — 10
Energy Level	1 — 10	1 — 10	1 — 10	1 — 10	1 — 10	1 — 10	1 — 10
Kept Focus	1 — 10	1 — 10	1 — 10	1 — 10	1 — 10	1 — 10	1 — 10
Able to complete tasks	1 — 10	1 — 10	1 — 10	1 — 10	1 — 10	1 — 10	1 — 10
Motivation level	1 — 10	1 — 10	1 — 10	1 — 10	1 — 10	1 — 10	1 — 10
Healthy appetite	1 — 10	1 — 10	1 — 10	1 — 10	1 — 10	1 — 10	1 — 10
Physical symptoms:							
• Headache	1 — 10	1 — 10	1 — 10	1 — 10	1 — 10	1 — 10	1 — 10
• Lethargy	1 — 10	1 — 10	1 — 10	1 — 10	1 — 10	1 — 10	1 — 10
• Nausea	1 — 10	1 — 10	1 — 10	1 — 10	1 — 10	1 — 10	1 — 10
• Other							
Notes							

REJECTION DYSPHORIA WORKSHEET

Date: _____

Time: _____

Where did the social interaction take place?
What exact words were said and by whom?
Then what exactly happened?

What did I think and how did I feel before I reacted to that?

What words did I use to respond? What was the effect of those words on the other person involved?

What was the outcome of this encounter?

If I felt rejected, how could I have reframed my thoughts to ward off that feeling?

Did I learn anything specific about myself or the other person?
Any ideas how to better approach my next social interaction?

ADHD Medication and BEHAVIOR Tracker

Week of: ___/___/___

	M	T	W	T	F	S	S
Initiate Social Contact							
Social Contact Results							
Medication Time & Dose							
Maintained Daily Routine							
Sleep and Rest hours							
Healthy Diet							
Exercise / Activity							

BEHAVIOR TRACKER

	M	T	W	T	F	S	S
Became Irritable	1 — 10	1 — 10	1 — 10	1 — 10	1 — 10	1 — 10	1 — 10
Felt Agitated	1 — 10	1 — 10	1 — 10	1 — 10	1 — 10	1 — 10	1 — 10
Unable to concentrate	1 — 10	1 — 10	1 — 10	1 — 10	1 — 10	1 — 10	1 — 10
Memory Loss	1 — 10	1 — 10	1 — 10	1 — 10	1 — 10	1 — 10	1 — 10
Energy Level	1 — 10	1 — 10	1 — 10	1 — 10	1 — 10	1 — 10	1 — 10
Kept Focus	1 — 10	1 — 10	1 — 10	1 — 10	1 — 10	1 — 10	1 — 10
Able to complete tasks	1 — 10	1 — 10	1 — 10	1 — 10	1 — 10	1 — 10	1 — 10
Motivation level	1 — 10	1 — 10	1 — 10	1 — 10	1 — 10	1 — 10	1 — 10
Healthy appetite	1 — 10	1 — 10	1 — 10	1 — 10	1 — 10	1 — 10	1 — 10
Physical symptoms:							
• Headache	1 — 10	1 — 10	1 — 10	1 — 10	1 — 10	1 — 10	1 — 10
• Lethargy	1 — 10	1 — 10	1 — 10	1 — 10	1 — 10	1 — 10	1 — 10
• Nausea	1 — 10	1 — 10	1 — 10	1 — 10	1 — 10	1 — 10	1 — 10
• Other							
Notes							

REJECTION DYSPHORIA WORKSHEET

Date: _____

Time: _____

Where did the social interaction take place?
What exact words were said and by whom?
Then what exactly happened?

What did I think and how did I feel before I reacted to that?

What words did I use to respond? What was the effect of those words on the other person involved?

What was the outcome of this encounter?

If I felt rejected, how could I have reframed my thoughts to ward off that feeling?

Did I learn anything specific about myself or the other person? Any ideas how to better approach my next social interaction?

ADHD Medication and
BEHAVIOR Tracker

Week of: ____/____/____

	M	T	W	T	F	S	S
Initiate Social Contact							
Social Contact Results							
Medication Time & Dose							
Maintained Daily Routine							
Sleep and Rest hours							
Healthy Diet							
Exercise / Activity							

BEHAVIOR TRACKER

	M	T	W	T	F	S	S
Became Irritable	1 — 10	1 — 10	1 — 10	1 — 10	1 — 10	1 — 10	1 — 10
Felt Agitated	1 — 10	1 — 10	1 — 10	1 — 10	1 — 10	1 — 10	1 — 10
Unable to concentrate	1 — 10	1 — 10	1 — 10	1 — 10	1 — 10	1 — 10	1 — 10
Memory Loss	1 — 10	1 — 10	1 — 10	1 — 10	1 — 10	1 — 10	1 — 10
Energy Level	1 — 10	1 — 10	1 — 10	1 — 10	1 — 10	1 — 10	1 — 10
Kept Focus	1 — 10	1 — 10	1 — 10	1 — 10	1 — 10	1 — 10	1 — 10
Able to complete tasks	1 — 10	1 — 10	1 — 10	1 — 10	1 — 10	1 — 10	1 — 10
Motivation level	1 — 10	1 — 10	1 — 10	1 — 10	1 — 10	1 — 10	1 — 10
Healthy appetite	1 — 10	1 — 10	1 — 10	1 — 10	1 — 10	1 — 10	1 — 10
Physical symptoms:							
• Headache	1 — 10	1 — 10	1 — 10	1 — 10	1 — 10	1 — 10	1 — 10
• Lethargy	1 — 10	1 — 10	1 — 10	1 — 10	1 — 10	1 — 10	1 — 10
• Nausea	1 — 10	1 — 10	1 — 10	1 — 10	1 — 10	1 — 10	1 — 10
• Other							
Notes							

REJECTION DYSPHORIA WORKSHEET

Date: _____

Time: _____

Where did the social interaction take place?
What exact words were said and by whom?
Then what exactly happened?

What did I think and how did I feel before I reacted to that?

What words did I use to respond? What was the effect of those words on the other person involved?

What was the outcome of this encounter?

If I felt rejected, how could I have reframed my thoughts to ward off that feeling?

Did I learn anything specific about myself or the other person? Any ideas how to better approach my next social interaction?

ADHD Medication and
BEHAVIOR Tracker

Week of: ____/____/____

	M	T	W	T	F	S	S
Initiate Social Contact							
Social Contact Results							
Medication Time & Dose							
Maintained Daily Routine							
Sleep and Rest hours							
Healthy Diet							
Exercise / Activity							

BEHAVIOR TRACKER

	M	T	W	T	F	S	S
Became Irritable	1 — 10	1 — 10	1 — 10	1 — 10	1 — 10	1 — 10	1 — 10
Felt Agitated	1 — 10	1 — 10	1 — 10	1 — 10	1 — 10	1 — 10	1 — 10
Unable to concentrate	1 — 10	1 — 10	1 — 10	1 — 10	1 — 10	1 — 10	1 — 10
Memory Loss	1 — 10	1 — 10	1 — 10	1 — 10	1 — 10	1 — 10	1 — 10
Energy Level	1 — 10	1 — 10	1 — 10	1 — 10	1 — 10	1 — 10	1 — 10
Kept Focus	1 — 10	1 — 10	1 — 10	1 — 10	1 — 10	1 — 10	1 — 10
Able to complete tasks	1 — 10	1 — 10	1 — 10	1 — 10	1 — 10	1 — 10	1 — 10
Motivation level	1 — 10	1 — 10	1 — 10	1 — 10	1 — 10	1 — 10	1 — 10
Healthy appetite	1 — 10	1 — 10	1 — 10	1 — 10	1 — 10	1 — 10	1 — 10
Physical symptoms:							
• Headache	1 — 10	1 — 10	1 — 10	1 — 10	1 — 10	1 — 10	1 — 10
• Lethargy	1 — 10	1 — 10	1 — 10	1 — 10	1 — 10	1 — 10	1 — 10
• Nausea	1 — 10	1 — 10	1 — 10	1 — 10	1 — 10	1 — 10	1 — 10
• Other							
Notes							

REJECTION DYSPHORIA WORKSHEET

Date: _____

Time: _____

Where did the social interaction take place?
What exact words were said and by whom?
Then what exactly happened?

What did I think and how did I feel before I reacted to that?

What words did I use to respond?
What was the effect of those words on the other person involved?

What was the outcome of this encounter?

If I felt rejected, how could I have reframed my thoughts to ward off that feeling?

Did I learn anything specific about myself or the other person?
Any ideas how to better approach my next social interaction?

ADHD Medication and
BEHAVIOR Tracker

Week of: _____ / _____ / _____

	M	T	W	T	F	S	S
Initiate Social Contact							
Social Contact Results							
Medication Time & Dose							
Maintained Daily Routine							
Sleep and Rest hours							
Healthy Diet							
Exercise / Activity							
BEHAVIOR TRACKER							
Became Irritable	1 — 10	1 — 10	1 — 10	1 — 10	1 — 10	1 — 10	1 — 10
Felt Agitated	1 — 10	1 — 10	1 — 10	1 — 10	1 — 10	1 — 10	1 — 10
Unable to concentrate	1 — 10	1 — 10	1 — 10	1 — 10	1 — 10	1 — 10	1 — 10
Memory Loss	1 — 10	1 — 10	1 — 10	1 — 10	1 — 10	1 — 10	1 — 10
Energy Level	1 — 10	1 — 10	1 — 10	1 — 10	1 — 10	1 — 10	1 — 10
Kept Focus	1 — 10	1 — 10	1 — 10	1 — 10	1 — 10	1 — 10	1 — 10
Able to complete tasks	1 — 10	1 — 10	1 — 10	1 — 10	1 — 10	1 — 10	1 — 10
Motivation level	1 — 10	1 — 10	1 — 10	1 — 10	1 — 10	1 — 10	1 — 10
Healthy appetite	1 — 10	1 — 10	1 — 10	1 — 10	1 — 10	1 — 10	1 — 10
Physical symptoms:							
• Headache	1 — 10	1 — 10	1 — 10	1 — 10	1 — 10	1 — 10	1 — 10
• Lethargy	1 — 10	1 — 10	1 — 10	1 — 10	1 — 10	1 — 10	1 — 10
• Nausea	1 — 10	1 — 10	1 — 10	1 — 10	1 — 10	1 — 10	1 — 10
• Other							
Notes							

REJECTION DYSPHORIA WORKSHEET

Date:
_____

Time:
_____

Where did the social interaction take place?
What exact words were said and by whom?
Then what exactly happened?

What did I think and how did I feel before I reacted to that?

What words did I use to respond? What was the effect of those words on the other person involved?

What was the outcome of this encounter?

If I felt rejected, how could I have reframed my thoughts to ward off that feeling?

Did I learn anything specific about myself or the other person? Any ideas how to better approach my next social interaction?

ADHD Medication and
BEHAVIOR Tracker

Week of: _____ / _____ / _____

	M	T	W	T	F	S	S
Initiate Social Contact							
Social Contact Results							
Medication Time & Dose							
Maintained Daily Routine							
Sleep and Rest hours							
Healthy Diet							
Exercise / Activity							

BEHAVIOR TRACKER

	M	T	W	T	F	S	S
Became Irritable	1 — 10	1 — 10	1 — 10	1 — 10	1 — 10	1 — 10	1 — 10
Felt Agitated	1 — 10	1 — 10	1 — 10	1 — 10	1 — 10	1 — 10	1 — 10
Unable to concentrate	1 — 10	1 — 10	1 — 10	1 — 10	1 — 10	1 — 10	1 — 10
Memory Loss	1 — 10	1 — 10	1 — 10	1 — 10	1 — 10	1 — 10	1 — 10
Energy Level	1 — 10	1 — 10	1 — 10	1 — 10	1 — 10	1 — 10	1 — 10
Kept Focus	1 — 10	1 — 10	1 — 10	1 — 10	1 — 10	1 — 10	1 — 10
Able to complete tasks	1 — 10	1 — 10	1 — 10	1 — 10	1 — 10	1 — 10	1 — 10
Motivation level	1 — 10	1 — 10	1 — 10	1 — 10	1 — 10	1 — 10	1 — 10
Healthy appetite	1 — 10	1 — 10	1 — 10	1 — 10	1 — 10	1 — 10	1 — 10
Physical symptoms:							
• Headache	1 — 10	1 — 10	1 — 10	1 — 10	1 — 10	1 — 10	1 — 10
• Lethargy	1 — 10	1 — 10	1 — 10	1 — 10	1 — 10	1 — 10	1 — 10
• Nausea	1 — 10	1 — 10	1 — 10	1 — 10	1 — 10	1 — 10	1 — 10
• Other							
Notes							

REJECTION DYSPHORIA WORKSHEET

Date: _____

Time: _____

Where did the social interaction take place?
What exact words were said and by whom?
Then what exactly happened?

What did I think and how did I feel before I reacted to that?

What words did I use to respond? What was the effect of those words on the other person involved?

What was the outcome of this encounter?

If I felt rejected, how could I have reframed my thoughts to ward off that feeling?

Did I learn anything specific about myself or the other person? Any ideas how to better approach my next social interaction?

ADHD Medication and
BEHAVIOR Tracker

Week of: ___/___/___

	M	T	W	T	F	S	S
Initiate Social Contact							
Social Contact Results							
Medication Time & Dose							
Maintained Daily Routine							
Sleep and Rest hours							
Healthy Diet							
Exercise / Activity							

BEHAVIOR TRACKER

	M	T	W	T	F	S	S
Became Irritable	1 — 10	1 — 10	1 — 10	1 — 10	1 — 10	1 — 10	1 — 10
Felt Agitated	1 — 10	1 — 10	1 — 10	1 — 10	1 — 10	1 — 10	1 — 10
Unable to concentrate	1 — 10	1 — 10	1 — 10	1 — 10	1 — 10	1 — 10	1 — 10
Memory Loss	1 — 10	1 — 10	1 — 10	1 — 10	1 — 10	1 — 10	1 — 10
Energy Level	1 — 10	1 — 10	1 — 10	1 — 10	1 — 10	1 — 10	1 — 10
Kept Focus	1 — 10	1 — 10	1 — 10	1 — 10	1 — 10	1 — 10	1 — 10
Able to complete tasks	1 — 10	1 — 10	1 — 10	1 — 10	1 — 10	1 — 10	1 — 10
Motivation level	1 — 10	1 — 10	1 — 10	1 — 10	1 — 10	1 — 10	1 — 10
Healthy appetite	1 — 10	1 — 10	1 — 10	1 — 10	1 — 10	1 — 10	1 — 10
Physical symptoms:							
• Headache	1 — 10	1 — 10	1 — 10	1 — 10	1 — 10	1 — 10	1 — 10
• Lethargy	1 — 10	1 — 10	1 — 10	1 — 10	1 — 10	1 — 10	1 — 10
• Nausea	1 — 10	1 — 10	1 — 10	1 — 10	1 — 10	1 — 10	1 — 10
• Other							
Notes							

REJECTION DYSPHORIA WORKSHEET

Date:

Time:

Where did the social interaction take place?
What exact words were said and by whom?
Then what exactly happened?

What did I think and how did I feel before I reacted to that?

What words did I use to respond? What was the effect of those words on the other person involved?

What was the outcome of this encounter?

If I felt rejected, how could I have reframed my thoughts to ward off that feeling?

Did I learn anything specific about myself or the other person? Any ideas how to better approach my next social interaction?

ADHD Medication and
BEHAVIOR Tracker

Week of:

____/____/____

	M	T	W	T	F	S	S
Initiate Social Contact							
Social Contact Results							
Medication Time & Dose							
Maintained Daily Routine							
Sleep and Rest hours							
Healthy Diet							
Exercise / Activity							
BEHAVIOR TRACKER							
Became Irritable	1 — 10	1 — 10	1 — 10	1 — 10	1 — 10	1 — 10	1 — 10
Felt Agitated	1 — 10	1 — 10	1 — 10	1 — 10	1 — 10	1 — 10	1 — 10
Unable to concentrate	1 — 10	1 — 10	1 — 10	1 — 10	1 — 10	1 — 10	1 — 10
Memory Loss	1 — 10	1 — 10	1 — 10	1 — 10	1 — 10	1 — 10	1 — 10
Energy Level	1 — 10	1 — 10	1 — 10	1 — 10	1 — 10	1 — 10	1 — 10
Kept Focus	1 — 10	1 — 10	1 — 10	1 — 10	1 — 10	1 — 10	1 — 10
Able to complete tasks	1 — 10	1 — 10	1 — 10	1 — 10	1 — 10	1 — 10	1 — 10
Motivation level	1 — 10	1 — 10	1 — 10	1 — 10	1 — 10	1 — 10	1 — 10
Healthy appetite	1 — 10	1 — 10	1 — 10	1 — 10	1 — 10	1 — 10	1 — 10
Physical symptoms:							
• Headache	1 — 10	1 — 10	1 — 10	1 — 10	1 — 10	1 — 10	1 — 10
• Lethargy	1 — 10	1 — 10	1 — 10	1 — 10	1 — 10	1 — 10	1 — 10
• Nausea	1 — 10	1 — 10	1 — 10	1 — 10	1 — 10	1 — 10	1 — 10
• Other							
Notes							

REJECTION DYSPHORIA WORKSHEET

Date: _____

Time: _____

Where did the social interaction take place?
What exact words were said and by whom?
Then what exactly happened?

What did I think and how did I feel before I reacted to that?

What words did I use to respond?
What was the effect of those words on the other person involved?

What was the outcome of this encounter?

If I felt rejected, how could I have reframed my thoughts to ward off that feeling?

Did I learn anything specific about myself or the other person?
Any ideas how to better approach my next social interaction?

ADHD Medication and
BEHAVIOR Tracker

Week of: _____/_____/_____

	M	T	W	T	F	S	S
Initiate Social Contact							
Social Contact Results							
Medication Time & Dose							
Maintained Daily Routine							
Sleep and Rest hours							
Healthy Diet							
Exercise / Activity							

BEHAVIOR TRACKER

	M	T	W	T	F	S	S
Became Irritable	1 — 10	1 — 10	1 — 10	1 — 10	1 — 10	1 — 10	1 — 10
Felt Agitated	1 — 10	1 — 10	1 — 10	1 — 10	1 — 10	1 — 10	1 — 10
Unable to concentrate	1 — 10	1 — 10	1 — 10	1 — 10	1 — 10	1 — 10	1 — 10
Memory Loss	1 — 10	1 — 10	1 — 10	1 — 10	1 — 10	1 — 10	1 — 10
Energy Level	1 — 10	1 — 10	1 — 10	1 — 10	1 — 10	1 — 10	1 — 10
Kept Focus	1 — 10	1 — 10	1 — 10	1 — 10	1 — 10	1 — 10	1 — 10
Able to complete tasks	1 — 10	1 — 10	1 — 10	1 — 10	1 — 10	1 — 10	1 — 10
Motivation level	1 — 10	1 — 10	1 — 10	1 — 10	1 — 10	1 — 10	1 — 10
Healthy appetite	1 — 10	1 — 10	1 — 10	1 — 10	1 — 10	1 — 10	1 — 10
Physical symptoms:							
• Headache	1 — 10	1 — 10	1 — 10	1 — 10	1 — 10	1 — 10	1 — 10
• Lethargy	1 — 10	1 — 10	1 — 10	1 — 10	1 — 10	1 — 10	1 — 10
• Nausea	1 — 10	1 — 10	1 — 10	1 — 10	1 — 10	1 — 10	1 — 10
• Other							
Notes							

REJECTION DYSPHORIA WORKSHEET

Where did the social interaction take place?
What exact words were said and by whom?
Then what exactly happened?

What did I think and how did I feel before I reacted to that?

What words did I use to respond? What was the effect of those words on the other person involved?

What was the outcome of this encounter?

If I felt rejected, how could I have reframed my thoughts to ward off that feeling?

Did I learn anything specific about myself or the other person? Any ideas how to better approach my next social interaction?

ADHD Medication and
BEHAVIOR Tracker

Week of:

____/____/____

	M	T	W	T	F	S	S
Initiate Social Contact							
Social Contact Results							
Medication Time & Dose							
Maintained Daily Routine							
Sleep and Rest hours							
Healthy Diet							
Exercise / Activity							
BEHAVIOR TRACKER							
Became Irritable	1 — 10	1 — 10	1 — 10	1 — 10	1 — 10	1 — 10	1 — 10
Felt Agitated	1 — 10	1 — 10	1 — 10	1 — 10	1 — 10	1 — 10	1 — 10
Unable to concentrate	1 — 10	1 — 10	1 — 10	1 — 10	1 — 10	1 — 10	1 — 10
Memory Loss	1 — 10	1 — 10	1 — 10	1 — 10	1 — 10	1 — 10	1 — 10
Energy Level	1 — 10	1 — 10	1 — 10	1 — 10	1 — 10	1 — 10	1 — 10
Kept Focus	1 — 10	1 — 10	1 — 10	1 — 10	1 — 10	1 — 10	1 — 10
Able to complete tasks	1 — 10	1 — 10	1 — 10	1 — 10	1 — 10	1 — 10	1 — 10
Motivation level	1 — 10	1 — 10	1 — 10	1 — 10	1 — 10	1 — 10	1 — 10
Healthy appetite	1 — 10	1 — 10	1 — 10	1 — 10	1 — 10	1 — 10	1 — 10
Physical symptoms:							
• Headache	1 — 10	1 — 10	1 — 10	1 — 10	1 — 10	1 — 10	1 — 10
• Lethargy	1 — 10	1 — 10	1 — 10	1 — 10	1 — 10	1 — 10	1 — 10
• Nausea	1 — 10	1 — 10	1 — 10	1 — 10	1 — 10	1 — 10	1 — 10
• Other							
Notes							

REJECTION DYSPHORIA WORKSHEET

Date: _____

Time: _____

Where did the social interaction take place?
What exact words were said and by whom?
Then what exactly happened?

What did I think and how did I feel before I reacted to that?

What words did I use to respond? What was the effect of those words on the other person involved?

What was the outcome of this encounter?

If I felt rejected, how could I have reframed my thoughts to ward off that feeling?

Did I learn anything specific about myself or the other person? Any ideas how to better approach my next social interaction?

ADHD Medication and
BEHAVIOR Tracker

Week of: ___/___/___

	M	T	W	T	F	S	S
Initiate Social Contact							
Social Contact Results							
Medication Time & Dose							
Maintained Daily Routine							
Sleep and Rest hours							
Healthy Diet							
Exercise / Activity							

BEHAVIOR TRACKER

	M	T	W	T	F	S	S
Became Irritable	1 — 10	1 — 10	1 — 10	1 — 10	1 — 10	1 — 10	1 — 10
Felt Agitated	1 — 10	1 — 10	1 — 10	1 — 10	1 — 10	1 — 10	1 — 10
Unable to concentrate	1 — 10	1 — 10	1 — 10	1 — 10	1 — 10	1 — 10	1 — 10
Memory Loss	1 — 10	1 — 10	1 — 10	1 — 10	1 — 10	1 — 10	1 — 10
Energy Level	1 — 10	1 — 10	1 — 10	1 — 10	1 — 10	1 — 10	1 — 10
Kept Focus	1 — 10	1 — 10	1 — 10	1 — 10	1 — 10	1 — 10	1 — 10
Able to complete tasks	1 — 10	1 — 10	1 — 10	1 — 10	1 — 10	1 — 10	1 — 10
Motivation level	1 — 10	1 — 10	1 — 10	1 — 10	1 — 10	1 — 10	1 — 10
Healthy appetite	1 — 10	1 — 10	1 — 10	1 — 10	1 — 10	1 — 10	1 — 10
Physical symptoms:							
• Headache	1 — 10	1 — 10	1 — 10	1 — 10	1 — 10	1 — 10	1 — 10
• Lethargy	1 — 10	1 — 10	1 — 10	1 — 10	1 — 10	1 — 10	1 — 10
• Nausea	1 — 10	1 — 10	1 — 10	1 — 10	1 — 10	1 — 10	1 — 10
• Other							
Notes							

REJECTION DYSPHORIA WORKSHEET

Date:
_____

Time:
_____

Where did the social interaction take place?
What exact words were said and by whom?
Then what exactly happened?

What did I think and how did I feel before I reacted to that?

What words did I use to respond? What was the effect of those words on the other person involved?

What was the outcome of this encounter?

If I felt rejected, how could I have reframed my thoughts to ward off that feeling?

Did I learn anything specific about myself or the other person?
Any ideas how to better approach my next social interaction?

ADHD Medication and
BEHAVIOR Tracker

Week of: ___ / ___ / ___

	M	T	W	T	F	S	S
Initiate Social Contact							
Social Contact Results							
Medication Time & Dose							
Maintained Daily Routine							
Sleep and Rest hours							
Healthy Diet							
Exercise / Activity							

BEHAVIOR TRACKER

	M	T	W	T	F	S	S
Became Irritable	1 — 10	1 — 10	1 — 10	1 — 10	1 — 10	1 — 10	1 — 10
Felt Agitated	1 — 10	1 — 10	1 — 10	1 — 10	1 — 10	1 — 10	1 — 10
Unable to concentrate	1 — 10	1 — 10	1 — 10	1 — 10	1 — 10	1 — 10	1 — 10
Memory Loss	1 — 10	1 — 10	1 — 10	1 — 10	1 — 10	1 — 10	1 — 10
Energy Level	1 — 10	1 — 10	1 — 10	1 — 10	1 — 10	1 — 10	1 — 10
Kept Focus	1 — 10	1 — 10	1 — 10	1 — 10	1 — 10	1 — 10	1 — 10
Able to complete tasks	1 — 10	1 — 10	1 — 10	1 — 10	1 — 10	1 — 10	1 — 10
Motivation level	1 — 10	1 — 10	1 — 10	1 — 10	1 — 10	1 — 10	1 — 10
Healthy appetite	1 — 10	1 — 10	1 — 10	1 — 10	1 — 10	1 — 10	1 — 10
Physical symptoms:							
• Headache	1 — 10	1 — 10	1 — 10	1 — 10	1 — 10	1 — 10	1 — 10
• Lethargy	1 — 10	1 — 10	1 — 10	1 — 10	1 — 10	1 — 10	1 — 10
• Nausea	1 — 10	1 — 10	1 — 10	1 — 10	1 — 10	1 — 10	1 — 10
• Other							
Notes							

REJECTION DYSPHORIA WORKSHEET

Date: _____

Time: _____

Where did the social interaction take place?
What exact words were said and by whom?
Then what exactly happened?

What did I think and how did I feel before I reacted to that?

What words did I use to respond? What was the effect of those words on the other person involved?

What was the outcome of this encounter?

If I felt rejected, how could I have reframed my thoughts to ward off that feeling?

Did I learn anything specific about myself or the other person? Any ideas how to better approach my next social interaction?

ADHD Medication and
BEHAVIOR Tracker

	M	T	W	T	F	S	S
Initiate Social Contact							
Social Contact Results							
Medication Time & Dose							
Maintained Daily Routine							
Sleep and Rest hours							
Healthy Diet							
Exercise / Activity							

BEHAVIOR TRACKER

	M	T	W	T	F	S	S
Became Irritable	1 — 10	1 — 10	1 — 10	1 — 10	1 — 10	1 — 10	1 — 10
Felt Agitated	1 — 10	1 — 10	1 — 10	1 — 10	1 — 10	1 — 10	1 — 10
Unable to concentrate	1 — 10	1 — 10	1 — 10	1 — 10	1 — 10	1 — 10	1 — 10
Memory Loss	1 — 10	1 — 10	1 — 10	1 — 10	1 — 10	1 — 10	1 — 10
Energy Level	1 — 10	1 — 10	1 — 10	1 — 10	1 — 10	1 — 10	1 — 10
Kept Focus	1 — 10	1 — 10	1 — 10	1 — 10	1 — 10	1 — 10	1 — 10
Able to complete tasks	1 — 10	1 — 10	1 — 10	1 — 10	1 — 10	1 — 10	1 — 10
Motivation level	1 — 10	1 — 10	1 — 10	1 — 10	1 — 10	1 — 10	1 — 10
Healthy appetite	1 — 10	1 — 10	1 — 10	1 — 10	1 — 10	1 — 10	1 — 10
Physical symptoms:							
• Headache	1 — 10	1 — 10	1 — 10	1 — 10	1 — 10	1 — 10	1 — 10
• Lethargy	1 — 10	1 — 10	1 — 10	1 — 10	1 — 10	1 — 10	1 — 10
• Nausea	1 — 10	1 — 10	1 — 10	1 — 10	1 — 10	1 — 10	1 — 10
• Other							
Notes							

REJECTION DYSPHORIA WORKSHEET

Date: _____

Time: _____

Where did the social interaction take place?
What exact words were said and by whom?
Then what exactly happened?

What did I think and how did I feel before I reacted to that?

What words did I use to respond? What was the effect of those words on the other person involved?

What was the outcome of this encounter?

If I felt rejected, how could I have reframed my thoughts to ward off that feeling?

Did I learn anything specific about myself or the other person? Any ideas how to better approach my next social interaction?

ADHD Medication and
BEHAVIOR Tracker

Week of:

_____/_____/_____

	M	T	W	T	F	S	S
Initiate Social Contact							
Social Contact Results							
Medication Time & Dose							
Maintained Daily Routine							
Sleep and Rest hours							
Healthy Diet							
Exercise / Activity							

BEHAVIOR TRACKER

	M	T	W	T	F	S	S
Became Irritable	1 — 10	1 — 10	1 — 10	1 — 10	1 — 10	1 — 10	1 — 10
Felt Agitated	1 — 10	1 — 10	1 — 10	1 — 10	1 — 10	1 — 10	1 — 10
Unable to concentrate	1 — 10	1 — 10	1 — 10	1 — 10	1 — 10	1 — 10	1 — 10
Memory Loss	1 — 10	1 — 10	1 — 10	1 — 10	1 — 10	1 — 10	1 — 10
Energy Level	1 — 10	1 — 10	1 — 10	1 — 10	1 — 10	1 — 10	1 — 10
Kept Focus	1 — 10	1 — 10	1 — 10	1 — 10	1 — 10	1 — 10	1 — 10
Able to complete tasks	1 — 10	1 — 10	1 — 10	1 — 10	1 — 10	1 — 10	1 — 10
Motivation level	1 — 10	1 — 10	1 — 10	1 — 10	1 — 10	1 — 10	1 — 10
Healthy appetite	1 — 10	1 — 10	1 — 10	1 — 10	1 — 10	1 — 10	1 — 10
Physical symptoms:							
• Headache	1 — 10	1 — 10	1 — 10	1 — 10	1 — 10	1 — 10	1 — 10
• Lethargy	1 — 10	1 — 10	1 — 10	1 — 10	1 — 10	1 — 10	1 — 10
• Nausea	1 — 10	1 — 10	1 — 10	1 — 10	1 — 10	1 — 10	1 — 10
• Other							
Notes							

REJECTION DYSPHORIA WORKSHEET

Date: _____

Time: _____

Where did the social interaction take place?
What exact words were said and by whom?
Then what exactly happened?

What did I think and how did I feel before I reacted to that?

What words did I use to respond? What was the effect of those words on the other person involved?

What was the outcome of this encounter?

If I felt rejected, how could I have reframed my thoughts to ward off that feeling?

Did I learn anything specific about myself or the other person?
Any ideas how to better approach my next social interaction?

ADHD Medication and
BEHAVIOR Tracker

	M	T	W	T	F	S	S
Initiate Social Contact							
Social Contact Results							
Medication Time & Dose							
Maintained Daily Routine							
Sleep and Rest hours							
Healthy Diet							
Exercise / Activity							

BEHAVIOR TRACKER

	M	T	W	T	F	S	S
Became Irritable	1 — 10	1 — 10	1 — 10	1 — 10	1 — 10	1 — 10	1 — 10
Felt Agitated	1 — 10	1 — 10	1 — 10	1 — 10	1 — 10	1 — 10	1 — 10
Unable to concentrate	1 — 10	1 — 10	1 — 10	1 — 10	1 — 10	1 — 10	1 — 10
Memory Loss	1 — 10	1 — 10	1 — 10	1 — 10	1 — 10	1 — 10	1 — 10
Energy Level	1 — 10	1 — 10	1 — 10	1 — 10	1 — 10	1 — 10	1 — 10
Kept Focus	1 — 10	1 — 10	1 — 10	1 — 10	1 — 10	1 — 10	1 — 10
Able to complete tasks	1 — 10	1 — 10	1 — 10	1 — 10	1 — 10	1 — 10	1 — 10
Motivation level	1 — 10	1 — 10	1 — 10	1 — 10	1 — 10	1 — 10	1 — 10
Healthy appetite	1 — 10	1 — 10	1 — 10	1 — 10	1 — 10	1 — 10	1 — 10
Physical symptoms:							
• Headache	1 — 10	1 — 10	1 — 10	1 — 10	1 — 10	1 — 10	1 — 10
• Lethargy	1 — 10	1 — 10	1 — 10	1 — 10	1 — 10	1 — 10	1 — 10
• Nausea	1 — 10	1 — 10	1 — 10	1 — 10	1 — 10	1 — 10	1 — 10
• Other							
Notes							

REJECTION DYSPHORIA WORKSHEET

Date: _____

Time: _____

Where did the social interaction take place?
What exact words were said and by whom?
Then what exactly happened?

What did I think and how did I feel before I reacted to that?

What words did I use to respond? What was the effect of those words on the other person involved?

What was the outcome of this encounter?

If I felt rejected, how could I have reframed my thoughts to ward off that feeling?

Did I learn anything specific about myself or the other person? Any ideas how to better approach my next social interaction?

ADHD Medication and
BEHAVIOR Tracker

Week of: ____ / ____ / ____

	M	T	W	T	F	S	S
Initiate Social Contact							
Social Contact Results							
Medication Time & Dose							
Maintained Daily Routine							
Sleep and Rest hours							
Healthy Diet							
Exercise / Activity							

BEHAVIOR TRACKER

	M	T	W	T	F	S	S
Became Irritable	1 — 10	1 — 10	1 — 10	1 — 10	1 — 10	1 — 10	1 — 10
Felt Agitated	1 — 10	1 — 10	1 — 10	1 — 10	1 — 10	1 — 10	1 — 10
Unable to concentrate	1 — 10	1 — 10	1 — 10	1 — 10	1 — 10	1 — 10	1 — 10
Memory Loss	1 — 10	1 — 10	1 — 10	1 — 10	1 — 10	1 — 10	1 — 10
Energy Level	1 — 10	1 — 10	1 — 10	1 — 10	1 — 10	1 — 10	1 — 10
Kept Focus	1 — 10	1 — 10	1 — 10	1 — 10	1 — 10	1 — 10	1 — 10
Able to complete tasks	1 — 10	1 — 10	1 — 10	1 — 10	1 — 10	1 — 10	1 — 10
Motivation level	1 — 10	1 — 10	1 — 10	1 — 10	1 — 10	1 — 10	1 — 10
Healthy appetite	1 — 10	1 — 10	1 — 10	1 — 10	1 — 10	1 — 10	1 — 10
Physical symptoms:							
• Headache	1 — 10	1 — 10	1 — 10	1 — 10	1 — 10	1 — 10	1 — 10
• Lethargy	1 — 10	1 — 10	1 — 10	1 — 10	1 — 10	1 — 10	1 — 10
• Nausea	1 — 10	1 — 10	1 — 10	1 — 10	1 — 10	1 — 10	1 — 10
• Other							
Notes							

REJECTION DYSPHORIA WORKSHEET

Date:

_____

Time:

_____

Where did the social interaction take place?
What exact words were said and by whom?
Then what exactly happened?

What did I think and how did I feel before I reacted to that?

What words did I use to respond? What was the effect of those words on the other person involved?

What was the outcome of this encounter?

If I felt rejected, how could I have reframed my thoughts to ward off that feeling?

Did I learn anything specific about myself or the other person?
Any ideas how to better approach my next social interaction?

ADHD Medication and
BEHAVIOR Tracker

Week of: _____ / _____ / _____

	M	T	W	T	F	S	S
Initiate Social Contact							
Social Contact Results							
Medication Time & Dose							
Maintained Daily Routine							
Sleep and Rest hours							
Healthy Diet							
Exercise / Activity							

BEHAVIOR TRACKER

	M	T	W	T	F	S	S
Became Irritable	1 — 10	1 — 10	1 — 10	1 — 10	1 — 10	1 — 10	1 — 10
Felt Agitated	1 — 10	1 — 10	1 — 10	1 — 10	1 — 10	1 — 10	1 — 10
Unable to concentrate	1 — 10	1 — 10	1 — 10	1 — 10	1 — 10	1 — 10	1 — 10
Memory Loss	1 — 10	1 — 10	1 — 10	1 — 10	1 — 10	1 — 10	1 — 10
Energy Level	1 — 10	1 — 10	1 — 10	1 — 10	1 — 10	1 — 10	1 — 10
Kept Focus	1 — 10	1 — 10	1 — 10	1 — 10	1 — 10	1 — 10	1 — 10
Able to complete tasks	1 — 10	1 — 10	1 — 10	1 — 10	1 — 10	1 — 10	1 — 10
Motivation level	1 — 10	1 — 10	1 — 10	1 — 10	1 — 10	1 — 10	1 — 10
Healthy appetite	1 — 10	1 — 10	1 — 10	1 — 10	1 — 10	1 — 10	1 — 10
Physical symptoms:							
• Headache	1 — 10	1 — 10	1 — 10	1 — 10	1 — 10	1 — 10	1 — 10
• Lethargy	1 — 10	1 — 10	1 — 10	1 — 10	1 — 10	1 — 10	1 — 10
• Nausea	1 — 10	1 — 10	1 — 10	1 — 10	1 — 10	1 — 10	1 — 10
• Other							
Notes							

REJECTION DYSPHORIA WORKSHEET

Date: _____

Time: _____

Where did the social interaction take place?
What exact words were said and by whom?
Then what exactly happened?

What did I think and how did I feel before I reacted to that?

What words did I use to respond? What was the effect of those words on the other person involved?

What was the outcome of this encounter?

If I felt rejected, how could I have reframed my thoughts to ward off that feeling?

Did I learn anything specific about myself or the other person? Any ideas how to better approach my next social interaction?

ADHD Medication and
BEHAVIOR Tracker

Week of: ____/____/____

	M	T	W	T	F	S	S
Initiate Social Contact							
Social Contact Results							
Medication Time & Dose							
Maintained Daily Routine							
Sleep and Rest hours							
Healthy Diet							
Exercise / Activity							

BEHAVIOR TRACKER

	M	T	W	T	F	S	S
Became Irritable	1 — 10	1 — 10	1 — 10	1 — 10	1 — 10	1 — 10	1 — 10
Felt Agitated	1 — 10	1 — 10	1 — 10	1 — 10	1 — 10	1 — 10	1 — 10
Unable to concentrate	1 — 10	1 — 10	1 — 10	1 — 10	1 — 10	1 — 10	1 — 10
Memory Loss	1 — 10	1 — 10	1 — 10	1 — 10	1 — 10	1 — 10	1 — 10
Energy Level	1 — 10	1 — 10	1 — 10	1 — 10	1 — 10	1 — 10	1 — 10
Kept Focus	1 — 10	1 — 10	1 — 10	1 — 10	1 — 10	1 — 10	1 — 10
Able to complete tasks	1 — 10	1 — 10	1 — 10	1 — 10	1 — 10	1 — 10	1 — 10
Motivation level	1 — 10	1 — 10	1 — 10	1 — 10	1 — 10	1 — 10	1 — 10
Healthy appetite	1 — 10	1 — 10	1 — 10	1 — 10	1 — 10	1 — 10	1 — 10
Physical symptoms:							
• Headache	1 — 10	1 — 10	1 — 10	1 — 10	1 — 10	1 — 10	1 — 10
• Lethargy	1 — 10	1 — 10	1 — 10	1 — 10	1 — 10	1 — 10	1 — 10
• Nausea	1 — 10	1 — 10	1 — 10	1 — 10	1 — 10	1 — 10	1 — 10
• Other							
Notes							

REJECTION DYSPHORIA WORKSHEET

Date: _____

Time: _____

Where did the social interaction take place?
What exact words were said and by whom?
Then what exactly happened?

What did I think and how did I feel before I reacted to that?

What words did I use to respond? What was the effect of those words on the other person involved?

What was the outcome of this encounter?

If I felt rejected, how could I have reframed my thoughts to ward off that feeling?

Did I learn anything specific about myself or the other person?
Any ideas how to better approach my next social interaction?

ADHD Medication and
BEHAVIOR Tracker

Week of:

____/____/____

	M	T	W	T	F	S	S
Initiate Social Contact							
Social Contact Results							
Medication Time & Dose							
Maintained Daily Routine							
Sleep and Rest hours							
Healthy Diet							
Exercise / Activity							
BEHAVIOR TRACKER							
Became Irritable	1 — 10	1 — 10	1 — 10	1 — 10	1 — 10	1 — 10	1 — 10
Felt Agitated	1 — 10	1 — 10	1 — 10	1 — 10	1 — 10	1 — 10	1 — 10
Unable to concentrate	1 — 10	1 — 10	1 — 10	1 — 10	1 — 10	1 — 10	1 — 10
Memory Loss	1 — 10	1 — 10	1 — 10	1 — 10	1 — 10	1 — 10	1 — 10
Energy Level	1 — 10	1 — 10	1 — 10	1 — 10	1 — 10	1 — 10	1 — 10
Kept Focus	1 — 10	1 — 10	1 — 10	1 — 10	1 — 10	1 — 10	1 — 10
Able to complete tasks	1 — 10	1 — 10	1 — 10	1 — 10	1 — 10	1 — 10	1 — 10
Motivation level	1 — 10	1 — 10	1 — 10	1 — 10	1 — 10	1 — 10	1 — 10
Healthy appetite	1 — 10	1 — 10	1 — 10	1 — 10	1 — 10	1 — 10	1 — 10
Physical symptoms:							
• Headache	1 — 10	1 — 10	1 — 10	1 — 10	1 — 10	1 — 10	1 — 10
• Lethargy	1 — 10	1 — 10	1 — 10	1 — 10	1 — 10	1 — 10	1 — 10
• Nausea	1 — 10	1 — 10	1 — 10	1 — 10	1 — 10	1 — 10	1 — 10
• Other							
Notes							

REJECTION DYSPHORIA WORKSHEET

Date:
_____

Time:
_____

Where did the social interaction take place?
What exact words were said and by whom?
Then what exactly happened?

What did I think and how did I feel before I reacted to that?

What words did I use to respond? What was the effect of those words on the other person involved?

What was the outcome of this encounter?

If I felt rejected, how could I have reframed my thoughts to ward off that feeling?

Did I learn anything specific about myself or the other person? Any ideas how to better approach my next social interaction?

ADHD Medication and
BEHAVIOR Tracker

Week of: ____/____/____

	M	T	W	T	F	S	S
Initiate Social Contact							
Social Contact Results							
Medication Time & Dose							
Maintained Daily Routine							
Sleep and Rest hours							
Healthy Diet							
Exercise / Activity							

BEHAVIOR TRACKER

	M	T	W	T	F	S	S
Became Irritable	1 — 10	1 — 10	1 — 10	1 — 10	1 — 10	1 — 10	1 — 10
Felt Agitated	1 — 10	1 — 10	1 — 10	1 — 10	1 — 10	1 — 10	1 — 10
Unable to concentrate	1 — 10	1 — 10	1 — 10	1 — 10	1 — 10	1 — 10	1 — 10
Memory Loss	1 — 10	1 — 10	1 — 10	1 — 10	1 — 10	1 — 10	1 — 10
Energy Level	1 — 10	1 — 10	1 — 10	1 — 10	1 — 10	1 — 10	1 — 10
Kept Focus	1 — 10	1 — 10	1 — 10	1 — 10	1 — 10	1 — 10	1 — 10
Able to complete tasks	1 — 10	1 — 10	1 — 10	1 — 10	1 — 10	1 — 10	1 — 10
Motivation level	1 — 10	1 — 10	1 — 10	1 — 10	1 — 10	1 — 10	1 — 10
Healthy appetite	1 — 10	1 — 10	1 — 10	1 — 10	1 — 10	1 — 10	1 — 10
Physical symptoms:							
• Headache	1 — 10	1 — 10	1 — 10	1 — 10	1 — 10	1 — 10	1 — 10
• Lethargy	1 — 10	1 — 10	1 — 10	1 — 10	1 — 10	1 — 10	1 — 10
• Nausea	1 — 10	1 — 10	1 — 10	1 — 10	1 — 10	1 — 10	1 — 10
• Other							
Notes							

REJECTION DYSPHORIA WORKSHEET

Date:

_____

Time:

_____

Where did the social interaction take place?
What exact words were said and by whom?
Then what exactly happened?

What did I think and how did I feel before I reacted to that?

What words did I use to respond?
What was the effect of those words on the other person involved?

What was the outcome of this encounter?

If I felt rejected, how could I have reframed my thoughts to ward off that feeling?

Did I learn anything specific about myself or the other person?
Any ideas how to better approach my next social interaction?

ADHD Medication and
BEHAVIOR Tracker

Week of: ____/____/____

	M	T	W	T	F	S	S
Initiate Social Contact							
Social Contact Results							
Medication Time & Dose							
Maintained Daily Routine							
Sleep and Rest hours							
Healthy Diet							
Exercise / Activity							

BEHAVIOR TRACKER

	M	T	W	T	F	S	S
Became Irritable	1 — 10	1 — 10	1 — 10	1 — 10	1 — 10	1 — 10	1 — 10
Felt Agitated	1 — 10	1 — 10	1 — 10	1 — 10	1 — 10	1 — 10	1 — 10
Unable to concentrate	1 — 10	1 — 10	1 — 10	1 — 10	1 — 10	1 — 10	1 — 10
Memory Loss	1 — 10	1 — 10	1 — 10	1 — 10	1 — 10	1 — 10	1 — 10
Energy Level	1 — 10	1 — 10	1 — 10	1 — 10	1 — 10	1 — 10	1 — 10
Kept Focus	1 — 10	1 — 10	1 — 10	1 — 10	1 — 10	1 — 10	1 — 10
Able to complete tasks	1 — 10	1 — 10	1 — 10	1 — 10	1 — 10	1 — 10	1 — 10
Motivation level	1 — 10	1 — 10	1 — 10	1 — 10	1 — 10	1 — 10	1 — 10
Healthy appetite	1 — 10	1 — 10	1 — 10	1 — 10	1 — 10	1 — 10	1 — 10
Physical symptoms:							
• Headache	1 — 10	1 — 10	1 — 10	1 — 10	1 — 10	1 — 10	1 — 10
• Lethargy	1 — 10	1 — 10	1 — 10	1 — 10	1 — 10	1 — 10	1 — 10
• Nausea	1 — 10	1 — 10	1 — 10	1 — 10	1 — 10	1 — 10	1 — 10
• Other							
Notes							

REJECTION DYSPHORIA WORKSHEET

Date: _____

Time: _____

Where did the social interaction take place?
What exact words were said and by whom?
Then what exactly happened?

What did I think and how did I feel before I reacted to that?

What words did I use to respond? What was the effect of those words on the other person involved?

What was the outcome of this encounter?

If I felt rejected, how could I have reframed my thoughts to ward off that feeling?

Did I learn anything specific about myself or the other person?
Any ideas how to better approach my next social interaction?

ADHD Medication and
BEHAVIOR Tracker

Week of: ___/___/___

	M	T	W	T	F	S	S
Initiate Social Contact							
Social Contact Results							
Medication Time & Dose							
Maintained Daily Routine							
Sleep and Rest hours							
Healthy Diet							
Exercise / Activity							

BEHAVIOR TRACKER

	M	T	W	T	F	S	S
Became Irritable	1 — 10	1 — 10	1 — 10	1 — 10	1 — 10	1 — 10	1 — 10
Felt Agitated	1 — 10	1 — 10	1 — 10	1 — 10	1 — 10	1 — 10	1 — 10
Unable to concentrate	1 — 10	1 — 10	1 — 10	1 — 10	1 — 10	1 — 10	1 — 10
Memory Loss	1 — 10	1 — 10	1 — 10	1 — 10	1 — 10	1 — 10	1 — 10
Energy Level	1 — 10	1 — 10	1 — 10	1 — 10	1 — 10	1 — 10	1 — 10
Kept Focus	1 — 10	1 — 10	1 — 10	1 — 10	1 — 10	1 — 10	1 — 10
Able to complete tasks	1 — 10	1 — 10	1 — 10	1 — 10	1 — 10	1 — 10	1 — 10
Motivation level	1 — 10	1 — 10	1 — 10	1 — 10	1 — 10	1 — 10	1 — 10
Healthy appetite	1 — 10	1 — 10	1 — 10	1 — 10	1 — 10	1 — 10	1 — 10
Physical symptoms:							
• Headache	1 — 10	1 — 10	1 — 10	1 — 10	1 — 10	1 — 10	1 — 10
• Lethargy	1 — 10	1 — 10	1 — 10	1 — 10	1 — 10	1 — 10	1 — 10
• Nausea	1 — 10	1 — 10	1 — 10	1 — 10	1 — 10	1 — 10	1 — 10
• Other							
Notes							

REJECTION DYSPHORIA WORKSHEET

Date: _____

Time: _____

Where did the social interaction take place?
What exact words were said and by whom?
Then what exactly happened?

What did I think and how did I feel before I reacted to that?

What words did I use to respond?
What was the effect of those words on the other person involved?

What was the outcome of this encounter?

If I felt rejected, how could I have reframed my thoughts to ward off that feeling?

Did I learn anything specific about myself or the other person?
Any ideas how to better approach my next social interaction?

Brainstorm or Sketch

MEDICAL APPOINTMENTS

Date	Time	Doctor	Contact
Reason for Visit		Questions	Outcome
			Medication Prescribed?
Notes			Treatment
			Follow up

Date	Time	Doctor	Contact
Reason for Visit		Questions	Outcome
			Medication Prescribed?
Notes			Treatment
			Follow up

Date	Time	Doctor	Contact
Reason for Visit		Questions	Outcome
			Medication Prescribed?
Notes			Treatment
			Follow up

MEDICAL APPOINTMENTS

Date	Time	Doctor	Contact
Reason for Visit		Questions	Outcome
			Medication Prescribed?
Notes			Treatment
			Follow up

Date	Time	Doctor	Contact
Reason for Visit		Questions	Outcome
			Medication Prescribed?
Notes			Treatment
			Follow up

Date	Time	Doctor	Contact
Reason for Visit		Questions	Outcome
			Medication Prescribed?
Notes			Treatment
			Follow up

MEDICAL APPOINTMENTS

Date	Time	Doctor	Contact
Reason for Visit		**Questions**	**Outcome**
			Medication Prescribed?
Notes			**Treatment**
			Follow up

Date	Time	Doctor	Contact
Reason for Visit		**Questions**	**Outcome**
			Medication Prescribed?
Notes			**Treatment**
			Follow up

Date	Time	Doctor	Contact
Reason for Visit		**Questions**	**Outcome**
			Medication Prescribed?
Notes			**Treatment**
			Follow up

MEDICAL APPOINTMENTS

Date	Time	Doctor	Contact

Reason for Visit	Questions	Outcome
		Medication Prescribed?

Notes	Treatment
	Follow up

Date	Time	Doctor	Contact

Reason for Visit	Questions	Outcome
		Medication Prescribed?

Notes	Treatment
	Follow up

Date	Time	Doctor	Contact

Reason for Visit	Questions	Outcome
		Medication Prescribed?

Notes	Treatment
	Follow up

Brainstorm or Sketch

Made in United States
Troutdale, OR
11/15/2024

24882927R00066